THE STORY OF MADRAS

THE
STORY OF MADRAS

BY

GLYN BARLOW, M.A.

GYAN

Published by

Gyan Publishing House
5, Ansari Road
Daryaganj, New Delhi-110002
Phone: 011-47034999, 9811692060
E-mail: books@gyanbooks.com

Distribution Network
gyanbooks.com
India, USA, Canada, UK, Australia

ISBN: 978-81-212-5853-1 (PB)
First Published, 1921

2nd Impression 2024

Printed at: Gyan Press, Delhi.

THE STORY OF MADRAS
Author: GLYN BARLOW

THE STORY OF MADRAS

Chepauk Palace.
(Southern half)

THE STORY OF MADRAS

BY

GLYN BARLOW, M.A.

WITH MAPS AND ILLUSTRATIONS
BY THE AUTHOR

HUMPHREY MILFORD
OXFORD UNIVERSITY PRESS
LONDON, BOMBAY, CALCUTTA, MADRAS
1921

PREFACE

This little book is not a "History of Madras," although it contains a good deal of Madras history; and it is not a "Guide to Madras," although it gives accounts of some of the principal buildings in the city. The book will have fulfilled its purpose if it helps the reader to realize that the City of Madras is a particularly interesting corner of the world. This fact is often forgotten; and even many of the people who live in Madras itself, and who are aware that Madras has played an important part in the making of India's history, are strangely uninterested in its historic remains. They are eloquent perhaps in denouncing the heat of Madras and its mosquitoes and the iniquities of its Cooum river; but they have never a word to say on its enchanting memorials of the past. Madras has memorials indeed. Madras is an historical museum, where the sightseer may spend many and many an hour—in street and in building—studying old-world exhibits, and living for the while in the fascinating past. Madras is not an ancient city; its foundation is not ascribed to some mythic king who ruled in mythic times; it has no hoary ruins, too old to be historic and too legendary to be inspiring. But Madras is old enough for its records to be romantic, and at the same time is young enough for its earliest accounts of itself to be—not unsatisfying fables, but interesting fact. The story of Madras fills an absorbing page of history, and the sights of Madras are well worthy of sympathetic interest—especially on the part of those whose lines of life are cast in the historic city itself or within the historic presidency of which it is the capital.

In the following pages certain places and events have been briefly described more than once with different details; any such repetitions are due to the fact that the Story of Madras has been told in a series of vignettes, appertaining to particular buildings or particular conditions, and each vignette had to be complete in itself. It is hoped that such repetitions will be of familiar interest, rather than tedious.

In respect of the facts that are recorded, apart from general history, I am indebted principally to the valuable Records of Fort St. George, which the Madras Government have been publishing, volume by volume, during several years, and which I have studied with interest since the first volume appeared. Of other works that I have consulted, I must specially mention Colonel Love's "Vestiges of Madras," which is a very mine of information.

G.B.

MADRAS, 1921.

CONTENTS

ILLUSTRATIONS

CHRONOLOGICAL NOTES

The East India Company established ... ... A.D. 1600

First English settlement, at Masulipatam 1611

Site of Madras acquired by Mr. Francis Day ... 1639

The acquisition confirmed at Chandragiri by the Hindu 'Lord of the Carnatic' 1639

The Hindu lord of the Carnatic (the Raja of Chandragiri) dethroned by the Mohammedan Sultan of Golconda ... 1646

The Company secure from Golconda a fresh title to their possessions ... ...

The Sultan of Golconda dethroned by the Moghul Emperor, Aurangzeb, who appoints a 'Nawab of the Carnatic' 1687

The Company secure from a representative of the Emperor a fresh title to their possessions ... ...

Da-ud Khan, Nawab of the Carnatic, invests Madras for three months, and is finally bought off 1702

In Europe, England and France are engaged in the War of the Austrian Succession 1740–1748

Dupleix, who is possessed with the idea of making France politically influential in India, is appointed Governor of Pondicherry 1742

In the war in Europe he sees an opportunity for fighting the English in India, and French forces under LaBourdonnais capture Madras 1746

Treaty of Aix-la-Chapelle, by which Madras is restored to the English 1748

Two Carnatic princes quarrel for the Nawabship ... 1749

The French and the English in South India join in the quarrel on opposite sides. In the name of the claimant whom the English supported, Clive captures Arcot, the capital of the Carnatic, and then defends the town against the rival claimant and his French supporters ... 1749

The French are defeated in the open field, and the struggle is at an end 1752

In Europe, England and France are engaged in the Seven Years' War 1756–1763

In India, Count Lally besieges Madras unsuccessfully for more than two months ... ... A.D. 1758–1759

The English defeat the French at Wandiwash ... 1760

The English capture Pondicherry 1761

Treaty of Paris, by which Pondicherry is restored to the French 1763

(The town was captured again in 1786 and in 1803).

Haidar Ali makes himself Sultan of Mysore about 1760, and reigns till his death, which occurred in ... 1781

Tipu, his son, succeeds him, and reigns till he is slain in defending his capital, Seringapatam, against an assault by the English 1799

(Madras was frequently disturbed by the raids of the father and of the son; and Tipu's death relieved the townsmen of constant anxiety.)

The Supreme Court of Judicature established at Madras. 1801

In default of an heir, the Carnatic 'lapses' to the Company 1855

The Madras Railway opened for traffic 1856

The Indian Mutiny 1857–1859

The Madras University instituted 1857

The High Court established 1861

CHAPTER I

BEFORE THE BEGINNING

Three hundred years ago, Madras, under the name of 'Madraspatnam' was a tiny rural village on the Coromandel Coast. Scattered about in the neighbourhood there were other rural villages, such as Egmore, Vepery, and Triplicane, which are crowded districts in the great city of Madras to-day. In Triplicane there was an ancient temple, a centre of pilgrimage, dating, like many village temples in India, from very distant times; this was the Parthasarathy temple, which is the 'Triplicane Temple' still. A little fishing village called Kuppam, lying directly on the seashore, sent out, even as Kuppam does now, its bold fishermen in their rickety catamarans in perilous pursuit of the spoils of the sea. There was one small town in the neighbourhood, namely, the Portuguese settlement at Mylapore, where the tall façades of the several churches, peeping over the trees, formed a landmark for the Portuguese ships that occasionally cast anchor in the roads.

Such was the scene in 1639, the year in which our story of Madras begins. The Portuguese had already been in India for nearly a century and a half; and under their early and able viceroys they had made themselves powerful. The stately city of Goa was the capital of their Indian dominions, and they had settlements at Cochin, Calicut, Mylapore, and elsewhere. But the influence of the Portuguese was now on the wane. For nearly a century they had been the only European power in India and the Eastern seas; but merchants in other European countries had marked with jealous eyes the rich profits that the Portuguese derived from their Eastern traffic, and competitors appeared in the field. First came the Dutch, who in India established themselves at Pulicat, some twenty-five miles north of Mylapore. Holland had lately thrown off the yoke of Spain, and was full of new-born vigour; and Dutch trade in the East—chiefly in the East India Islands—was pushed with a rancorous energy that roused the vain indignation of the decadent Portuguese. Six years later, in 1600, came the English. The English traders were employees of the newly-established East India Company, and were sent out to do business for the Company in the East; and they had to face the opposition of the Dutch as well as of the Portuguese. Their earliest enterprise was in the East India Islands, and it was eleven years before they gained their first footing in India, at Masulipatam. Here they established an agency and did very considerable business; later they formed a fortified sub-agency at Armagaum, a good way down the coast, not far from Nellore. At first their fortunes went well; but local rulers exacted ruinous dues, and at Armagaum in particular the local ruler, alarmed at the influence that the English merchants had gained, set himself so seriously to the work of handicapping their trade that Mr. Francis Day, the Company's representative at Armagaum and a member of the Masulipatam Council, proposed to the Council that he should be allowed to seek a field for commercial enterprise more favourable than either Armagaum or Masulipatam. To Mr. Francis Day was committed the business of finding a suitable spot for a fresh settlement.

It was an important commission. The East India Company's existence depended entirely upon the profits of their trade. The Company's enterprise at Armagaum was hopeless; at Masulipatam it was very unsatisfactory; and Mr. Francis Day was appointed to find a place where the commercial prospects would be bright.

It should always be remembered that the East India Company was established purely as a commercial association, with its head office in London, and that its employees in India were men with business qualifications, appointed to carry on the Company's trade. The prime concern even of an Agent or a Governor was the making of good bargains on the Company's behalf—and sometimes on his own—getting the best prices for European broadcloths and brocades, and buying as cheaply as possible Indian muslins and calicoes and natural produce, for exportation to London, where they were sold at a large profit. Any fighting in which the Company's servants engaged was merely incidental to the pursuit of business in a land in which the ruling sovereigns, as well as the many small chiefs, were constantly at war. It is a maxim that 'Trade follows the Flag;' but in the case of India the Flag has followed Trade.

It is as a commercial man, therefore, that we must picture Mr. Francis Day setting out on his commercial mission; but it can be imagined that the English merchant, starting on an expedition in which he would be likely to seek personal interviews with rajas and nawabs and bid for their favour, set out in such style as would do the Company credit. In our mind's eye we picture Master Francis Day, Chief of Armagaum, standing on the deck of one of the Company's vessels lying at anchor in the Armagaum roads, and receiving his colleagues' farewells. His garb is that of a substantial merchant in the days of King Charles I. It has none of the extravagances that were the fashionable affectations of gay Cavaliers, but its sobriety makes it none the less smart. He wears a purple doublet and hose, a broad white collar edged with lace, and a gracefully-short black-velvet cloak. Curly hair falls beneath his broad-brimmed black hat, but not in long and scented ringlets such as were trained to fall below the shoulders of fashionable gallants at King Charles's court. He is in every way a fitting representative of the Honourable Company.

The bo'sun has piped his whistle, and the last good-byes have been said. The anchor's weighed, and the white sails are spread to the breeze. Master Day waves his hand to his colleagues in the surf-boat which is taking them shoreward, and the ship is headed to the south. The expedition is important—yes, and it was much more important than Master Day imagined; for something more serious than profits on muslin and brocade was on the anvil of fate.

CHAPTER II

THE BEGINNING

Mr. Francis Day was not sailing southward without definite plans. As the result of enquiries for a promising spot for a new settlement, it was his purpose to see if there was a favourable site in the neighbourhood of the old established Portuguese settlement at Mylapore. The Portuguese authorities at Mylapore, with whom Mr. Day seems to have corresponded, were not unwilling to have English neighbours. The ill-success of the English merchants at Masulipatam had probably allayed any fears that they would be formidable rivals to Portuguese trade at Mylapore; and furthermore the Portuguese welcomed the idea of European neighbours who would be at one with them in opposition to the forceful Dutchmen at Pulicat, up the coast, who showed no respect, not even of a ceremonious kind, for any vested interests—commercial or administrative—to which the Portuguese laid claim.

So Mr. Francis Day's vessel, standing no doubt well out to sea as it sailed past the foreshore of the Pulicat lagoon with its unfriendly Dutchmen, kept its course till the Mylapore churches were sighted and showed that the place where the first inquiries were to be made had been reached. The sails were furled and the anchors were dropped, and we may imagine that a salute was fired in honour of the King of Portugal, and was duly acknowledged.

It was in winter that Mr. Francis Day arrived—a time of the year when Madras looks its best and when the sea-horses are not always at their wildest tricks; and

Mr. Francis Day landed without accident, and was pleased with the scene. There are always breakers, however, on the Coromandel Coast, and Mr. Day found the landing so exciting that in his report to the Council at Masulipatam he wrote of 'the heavy and dangerous surf'. But after an inspection of the surroundings he was satisfied with the conditions; he considered that at the mouth of the Cooum river there was an advantageous site for a commercial settlement; and the local ruler, the Naik of Poonamallee, following the advice of the Portuguese authorities, encouraged him in the idea of an English settlement within the Poonamallee domain.

It is not surprising that Mr. Francis Day was pleased with what he saw; for Madras is not without beauty. In those idyllic days, moreover, the Cooum river, which was known then as the Triplicane river—and which even to-day can be beautiful, although for the greater part of the year it is no more than a stagnant ditch—must have been a limpid water-way; and to Mr. Francis Day, seeing it in winter, in which season the current swollen by the rain sometimes succeeds in bursting the bar, it must have appeared almost as a noble river, rushing down to the great sea—a river such as might well have deserved the erection of a town on its banks. The fact that the Portuguese had been at Mylapore for more than a century showed that a settlement was full of promise—and the more so for men with the energy of the English Company's representatives; and the conditions were such that Mr. Francis Day felt himself justified in entering into negotiations with the Naik for the grant of an estate extending five miles along the shore and a mile inland.

The negotiations were successful: but the Naik was subordinate to the lord of the soil, the Raja of Chandragiri, who was the living representative of the once great and magnificent Hindu empire of Vijianagar; and any grant that was made by the Naik of Poonamallee had to be confirmed by the Raja if it was to be made valid. Two or three miles from Chandragiri station, on the Katpadi-Gudur line of railway, is still to be seen the Rajah-Mahal, the palace in which the Raja handed to Mr. Francis Day the formal title to the land. The palace still exists, and it is a fine building, though partly in ruins. It is constructed entirely of granite, without any woodwork whatsoever; but its abounding interest lies not in its structure but in the fact that it was in this palace that the British Empire in India may be said to have been begotten.

There is no little interest in the thought that it was the Raja of Chandragiri that delivered the deed of possession to Mr. Francis Day. The Raja was an obscure representative of a magnificent Indian Empire of the past; Mr. Francis Day was an obscure representative of a magnificent Indian Empire that was yet to be; and the document that the Raja handed to Mr. Francis Day was in reality a patent of Empire, transferred from Vijianagar to Great Britain. It was at Chandragiri that the British Empire in India was begotten; it was at Madras that the British Empire was born.

Mr. Francis Day had fulfilled his mission. He had secured territory where the conditions seemed to give promise of success; and his work was approved. His superior officer, Mr. Andrew Cogan, Agent at Masulipatam, came away from Masulipatam to take charge of Madras, and with the co-operation of Mr. Francis Day he set about the development of the Company's new possession.

Of Mr. Francis Day's personal history we know little or nothing except that he was one of the Company's employees, and that he founded first an unsuccessful settlement at Armagaum—represented to-day by no more than a lighthouse—and afterwards a successful settlement at Madras. Later he was put in charge of the second settlement that he had founded, but he was relieved of, or resigned, the office at the end of a year. He then went to the Company's head-quarters at Bantam, in Java, and afterwards to England. What finally became of him is apparently unknown.

It would probably be difficult to say whether Mr. Francis Day was a great man with great ideals, or was merely a shrewd man of business, reliable for an important commercial mission. Remembering that the Company was strictly a commercial concern, we may think it likely that, in fixing upon Madras as a site for the Company's business, he was guided almost entirely by the question of trade-profits, and that in his mind's eye there were no prophetic visions of imperial glory. And it has been asked indeed whether or not he really chose well in choosing Madraspatnam by the Triplicane river as the site of the proposed new settlement; for there are those who have argued that the prosperity of Madras has been due to dogged British enterprise and placid Indian co-operation, not to natural advantages, and that Madras has prospered in spite of Madras. We must bear in mind, however, the limited geographical knowledge of the times and the limitations to Mr. Francis Day's choice; and, whatever the verdict may be, the fact remains that the Madraspatnam of Mr. Francis Day's selection is now a vast city, and that the Empire of India which was born at Chandragiri is now a mighty institution.

CHAPTER III

FORT ST. GEORGE

When the tract of land at Madras had been formally acquired, the European colony at Armagaum was forthwith shipped thereto (February, 1640). According to accounts, the colony, with Mr. Andrew Cogan at the head, assisted by Mr. Francis Day and perhaps another chief official, included some three or four British 'writers,' a gunner, a surgeon, a garrison of some twenty-five British soldiers under a lieutenant and a sergeant, a certain number of English carpenters, blacksmiths and coopers, and a small staff of English servants for kitchen and general work.

'Madras was a sandy beach . . . where the English began by erecting straw huts.' So says an old-time chronicle,[1] the work of an early resident of Madras; and, if we take the word 'straw' in a broad sense, we can easily conceive the scene. In Madras the bamboo and the palmyra grow in abundance, furnishing materials for the quick provision of cheap and commodious accommodation; and we can picture the pilgrim fathers of Madras camped in palmyra-thatched mat-sheds on the north bank of the Cooum river, near the bar, the while that the houses within the plan of the fort are being built.

[1] The chronicle was written by Manucci, an Italian doctor of an adventurous disposition, who, after varied and surprising experiences in northern India, settled down in Madras in 1686, and married a Eurasian widow. 'Manucci's Garden,' where he lived, covered a large area which is now occupied by a number of the houses at the Law College end of Popham's Broadway, on the side that is nearest the sea. The garden was watered by a stream that used to flow where the Broadway tram-lines now hold their course. *Vide* map, p. 10.

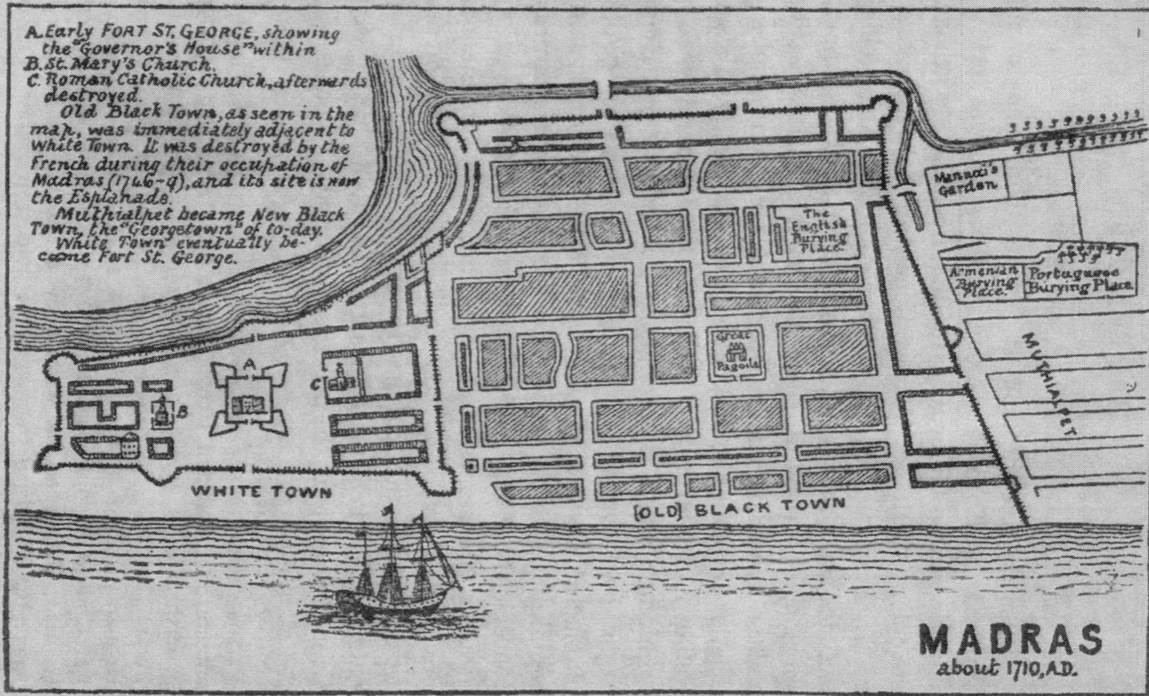
A. Early FORT ST. GEORGE, showing the "Governor's House" within
B. St. Mary's Church.
C. Roman Catholic Church, afterwards destroyed.
Old Black Town, as seen in the map, was immediately adjacent to White Town. It was destroyed by the French during their occupation of Madras (1746-9), and its site is now the Esplanade.
Muthialpet became New Black Town, the "Georgetown" of to-day.
White Town eventually became Fort St. George.
The English Burying Place.
Armenian Burying Place.
Portuguese Burying Place
Great Pagoda
MUTHIALPET
WHITE TOWN
(OLD) BLACK TOWN
MADRAS
about 1710, A.D.

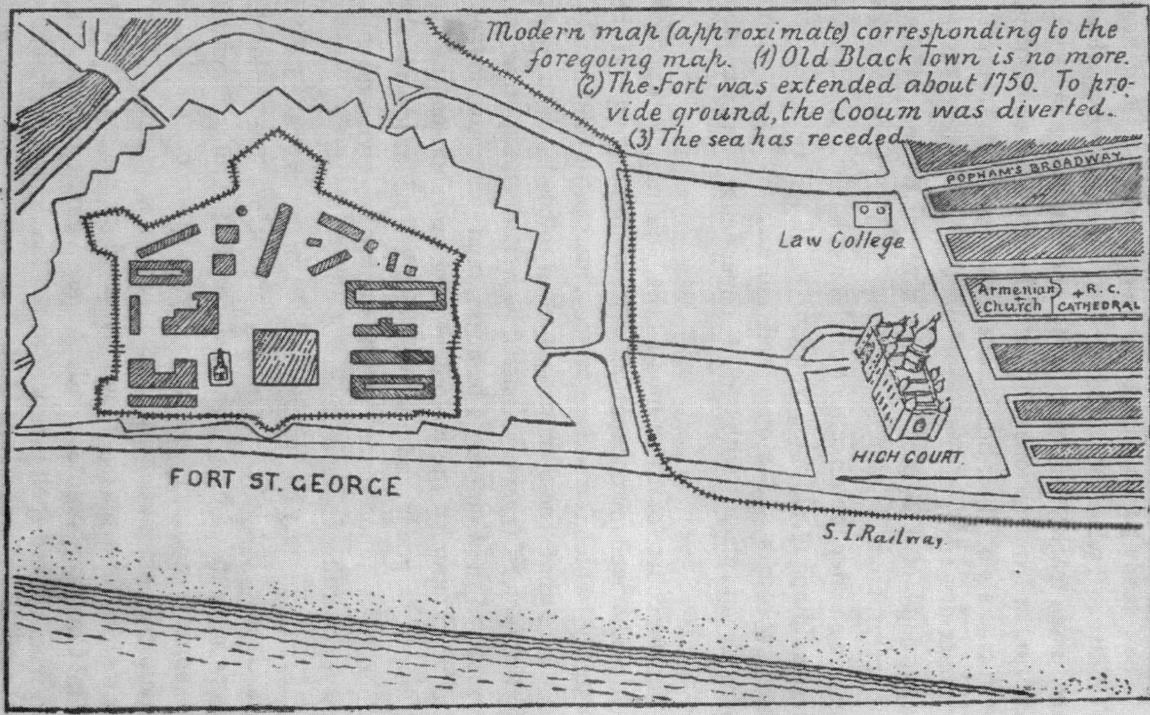
Modern map (approximate) corresponding to the foregoing map. (1) Old Black Town is no more. (2) The Fort was extended about 1750. To provide ground, the Cooum was diverted. (3) The sea has receded.
POPHAM'S BROADWAY
Law College
Armenian Church
R. C. CATHEDRAL
HIGH COURT
FORT ST. GEORGE
S. I. Railway

The 'sandy beach' has been waked from its longaeval placidity. Trains of bullock-carts are lumbering along new-made tracks, bringing stone and laterite and bricks and timber from various centres; and endless files of coolies, with baskets on their heads, are bringing sand from the summer-dry edges of the bed of the Cooum river. In the foreground of the picture, scores of chattering village-labourers, from Triplicane and other hamlets hard by, are working under the directions of the mechanical employees of the Company, chipping stone, mixing lime, sawing timber, carrying bricks and stones and mortar, or laying them adroitly in place, with little dependence on line and level.

In the course of a few months the buildings were sufficiently advanced for occupation. The main building was the 'factory,' which formerly signified a mercantile office; and it was here that the Company's chief officials, who were styled 'factors' (agents), assisted by writers and apprentices, transacted the Company's business, and were also lodged. Included amongst the buildings were warehouses for the Company's goods, and also barrack-like residences for the Company's subordinate British employees, civil and military, according to their rank.

From the very beginning the settlement was called Fort St. George, but it was several years before the buildings were surrounded by a high and fortified wall. It was in no spirit of military aggression that the Company's agents enclosed their settlement with a bastioned rampart, from whose battlements big cannon frowned on all sides round. The Company's representatives were 'gentle merchaunts,' to whom peace spelt prosperity ; but the times were lawless, and the gentle merchants were wise enough to recognize that days might come when it would be necessary to defend their merchandise and themselves, as well as the town of Madras, from the roving robber or the princely raider or the revengeful trade-rival, and that military preparedness was a dictate of prudence. The days came!

On such occasions the excitement in Fort St. George must have been great. We can imagine the anxiety with which, when the sentry gave the alarm, the gentle merchants climbed upon the walls and looked out at the horsemen that were to be descried in the distance, and asked one another disconsolately whether it was in peace or in war that they came. A brief notice of some of the occasions on which the Fort was in danger will be interesting.

Some fifty years after the Fort had been founded, a party of soldiers under the Commander-in-Chief of the Mohammedan King of Golconda pursued some of the King's enemies into Madras, "burning and Robbing of houses, and taking the Companies Cloth and goods," whereupon the Governor of the Fort sent them word that "he would use means to force them out of the Towne: Uppon which they retreated out of shott of the Fort." They returned, however, with additional strength, and for eight months they besieged the stronghold, but without success; and then they wearied of their hopeless endeavour, and march d away.

Later, a Dutch force, supported by Mohammedan cavalry, besieged San Thomé, which was then in the hands of the French; and for the purpose of the siege they occupied Triplicane village, mounting their cannon within the walls of Triplicane Temple, which they used as a fort. During the several weeks of the siege of San Thomé a powerful Dutch squadron blockaded the coast of Madras; and, as Britain and Holland were at war in Europe, there was constant anxiety in Fort St. George; but the Dutchmen contented themselves with the capture of San Thomé, and were prudent enough to let Fort St. George alone.

In the days of Queen Anne, Da-ud Khan, Nawab of the Carnatic, at the head of a large force, was reported to be marching to Madras. In Fort St. George there was much anxiety as to the purpose of his visit, and 'By order of the Governor and Council' various protective measures were immediately proclaimed. The proclamation is to be found in full in the Company's Minutes; and we find an amusing reminder of the Company's mercantile *raison d'être* in the fact that immediately after the military edicts comes the order 'That all the Company's cloth be brought from the washers, washed and unwashed, to prevent its being plundered.' The Nawab came, and he uttered threats, but he was mollified with luxurious entertainment. Inviting himself and his dewan and his chamberlain to dinner with the Governor and Councillors in the Fort, he was received with imposing honours, and was feasted in the Council Chamber at a magnificent banquet. The minutes relate that after dinner he was "diverted with the dancing wenches," and finally he got "very Drunk." At breakfast the next day in the Company's 'Garden,' His Highness again got "very drunk and fell a Sleep;" and a few days later he marched his army away. In his sober moments, however, he had been slyly measuring the Company's strength; and six months later he came back with a larger force, and blockaded Madras. He plundered all that he could, and on one occasion his spoil included "40 ox loads of the Company's cloth." For more than three months the blockade continued, and the Company's trade was entirely stopped, and provisions in Madras were exceedingly scarce. Da-ud Khan, eventually wearying of the unsuccessful siege, named the price that would buy him off; and the Council, fearing the wrath of the Directors at the loss of their trade, were glad to come to terms. The Company's Minute on the occasion is a brief but exultant record: 'The siege is raised!.'

In 1746 there was a siege of a more serious sort. England and France were at war in Europe, and suddenly a squadron of French ships appeared off Fort St. George. After a week's siege, the English merchants capitulated to superior force, and they were all sent to Pondicherry as prisoners, and the French flag waved over Madras; but by the treaty which ended the war, Madras was restored to the Company. Twelve years later Madras was once more besieged by the French, but unsuccessfully, and eventually the French leaders marched their forces away, quarrelling among themselves over their ill-success.

On several occasions, bodies of horsemen in the service of the adventurous Haidar Ali of Mysore, raided the country almost up to the Fort ditch, and were sometimes to be seen shaking their spears in defiance at the sentries on its walls.

These were not the only occasions on which Fort St. George was assailed, but they suffice to show how necessary it was that the Company's employees and their wares should be housed within the walls of a fort.

Fort St. George in the beginning was very small. Its external length parallel with the seashore was 108 yards, and its breadth was 100 yards. When White Town, which grew up around it, was fortified, there was 'a fort within a fort' (*vide* Map, p. 10); but eventually the inner wall was demolished. At various times the outer wall has been altered, but the Fort as we have it to-day is the self-same Fort St. George nevertheless, a glorious relic of by-gone times, and verily a history in stone.

The gates of Fort St. George open towards main thoroughfares of Madras, and it is permitted to anybody to pass in and out; but it is not visited nearly so much as its historic associations deserve. Let us pass within, and see if we cannot catch something like inspiration from the scene where so much history has been made, and where a great Empire was born.

An old-world feeling comes over us directly we leave the highroad and make our way down the sloped passage and across the drawbridge over the moat, past the massive gates and under the echoing tunnel that leads through the mighty walls. Within we see the parapets on which in bygone days the cannon thundered at the foe. We pass on into the great spaces of the Fort; and in our imagination

CLIVE'S HOUSE

we can people them with ghosts of the illustrious—or notorious—dead. It was here that, in the reign of King James the Second, Master Elihu Yale assumed the Governorship of Madras, did hard work in the Company's behalf but also made a large fortune for himself, lost his son aged four, quarrelled long and bitterly with his councillors, and was at last superseded. It was here that

Robert Clive, aged nineteen, newly arrived from England, entered upon his duties as an apprenticed writer in the Company's service, at a salary of five pounds per annum; it was here, in St. Mary's Church, eight years later, when he had won his first laurels, that he married the sister of one of the fellow-writers of his griffinhood; and it was here, in 'Clive's House,' which is still to be seen (now the Office of the Accountant-General), that he lived with his wife. The ancient Council Chamber is replete with historic associations; and St. Mary's Church offers material for many researchful and meditative visits. The streets have history in their names. 'Charles-and James Street,' for example, which is a present-day combination of two streets of yore, is jointly commemorative of the days of the Merry Monarch and of his royal but unfortunate brother. Enough! It is not my purpose to produce a guide-book to Madras, but to promote an appreciation of the historic interests of the city; and I take it that the reader has realized that Fort St. George is interesting indeed.

CHAPTER IV

DEVELOPMENT

When an English colony had settled down in Fort St. George, it was only to be expected that a town would spring up outside. The personal necessities of the numerous colonists had to be supplied, and purveyors and bazaarmen and workmen made themselves readily available for the supply. The requirements in respect of the Company's mercantile business were yet greater. The Company's agents wanted not only native employees in their office—'dubashes' and 'shroffs' and clerks and interpreters and porters and peons, but they also wanted wholesale buyers of the cloth and other articles that they imported from England for sale, and also merchants who could supply them with large quantities of the Indian wares that the Company exported to England; and they were able to get the men that they wanted.

A crowd attracts a crowd; and when once a town has begun to grow, it goes on growing of its own accord; and ten years after the acquisition of Madras, the population of the town was estimated at as many as 15,000 souls. The Fort itself, moreover, had to be enlarged; for the growth of the Company's business meant that more and more factors and writers had to be brought out from England, and more and more warehouses had to be provided for the multiplied wares; and, moreover, the increasing lawlessness of the times necessitated a larger garrison. Outside the Fort, Indian and other immigrants flocked from near and far to settle down within the Company's domains, looking for profit under the white men's protection; and, with their enterprising spirit, they played no small part in the development of Madras.

The town that grew up outside the little fort was divided into two sections—'the White Town' and 'the Black Town.' The boundaries of White Town corresponded roughly with what are now the boundaries of Fort St. George itself. The original Black Town—'Old Black Town'—covered what is now the vacant ground that lies between the Fort and the Law College, and included what are now the sites of the Law College and the High Court (*vide* Map, p. 10). The inhabitants of White Town included any British settlers not in the Company's service whose presence the Company approved, also all approved Portuguese and Eurasian immigrants from Mylapore, and a certain number of approved Indian Christians. White Town indeed was sometimes called the 'Christian Town.' Black Town was the Asiatic settlement. The great majority of the original Indian settlers were not Tamilians but Telugus—written down as 'Gentoos' in the Company's Records.

The Company's agents encouraged people of various races to reside in Madras; and the names of some of the streets and districts of the town are interesting testimonies as to the variety of the people who came.

Armenian Street—which began as an Armenian burial-ground (*vide* Map, p. 10)—is an example. Armenians from Persia, like their fellow-countrymen the Parsees, have a racial gift for commerce; and Armenian merchants had been in India long before the English arrived. Enterprising Armenian merchants settled in Madras in its early days to trade with the English colonists, and the Company's agents were glad to have as middlemen such able merchants who were in close touch with the people of the land. The most celebrated of the earlier Armenians in Madras was Peter Uscan, Armenian by race but Roman Catholic in religion, who lived in Madras for more than forty years, till his death there in 1751, at the age of seventy. He was a rich and public-spirited merchant. He built the Marmalong Bridge over the Adyar river, on one of the pillars of which a quaint inscription is still to be read, and he left a fund for its maintenance; he also renewed the multitude of stone steps that lead up to the top of St. Thomas's Mount. His inscribed tomb is to be seen in the churchyard of the Anglican Church of St. Matthias, Vepery, which in olden days was the chuchyard of a Roman Catholic chapel. Within the last half-century the Armenian community in Madras has been rapidly declining, as the result, probably, of inability to cope with the hustling style of commercial competition in these latter days; and only a very few representatives of the race are now to be seen in the city.

In Mint Street there is a small enclosure which is the remains of what was once a Jewish cemetery of considerable size; and the graves that are still to be seen are interesting reminders of the fact that in bygone times there was a Hebrew colony in Madras. In more than one of the Company's old records the Jews in Madras are referred to as being rich men, some of whom held positions of high civic authority. Some of them were English Jews, and others were Portuguese; and most of them were diamond merchants, on the look-out for diamonds from the mines of Golconda, which were formerly very productive. The English Jews exported diamonds to England, and imported silver and coral to Madras; coral was in great demand in India, and was sent out by Jewish firms in London. There is still a 'Coral Merchants' Street' in Madras, a continuation of Armenian Street, and it is a living reminder of the old Jewish colony. The Golconda mines eventually ceased to be productive, and Jewish diamond merchants are no longer to be seen in the city, and the Jewish colony has long since disappeared. Jews are notorious all the world over as money-lenders, and it may perhaps be wondered why none of them survived as money-lenders in Madras; but the fact that Coral Merchants' Street is now the habitat of Nattukottai Chetties, who are past-masters in the art of money-lending, suggests that even the Jews were unable to compete with Madras sowcars in the business of usury, and that the Chetties displaced the Jews who used to live in the street. The little Jewish cemetery in crowded Mint Street is an interesting spot. One of the antique tomb-stones has been caught in the branch of a tree and has been lifted high in air, and is a quaint sight; and the deserted little Hebrew graveyard itself is symbolic of the dispersion of the ancient people.

It is a curious fact that the Company's employees in South India never spoke of Indian Mohammedans as Mohammedans or as Moslems or as Mussalmans, but always as 'Moors.' It is thus that the name of 'Moor Street' is to be accounted for. The original 'Moors Street' was a street in which Mohammedans used to live, and the fact that one particular street in a large city should have borne such a name is evidence of another fact, namely, that in the earlier years of Madras very few Mohammedans resided in the town. It should be remembered that Madraspatnam, Triplicane, Egmore, and the other hamlets that went to make up the city of Madras were all of them Hindu villages; and it was only now and again that Mohammedans, in some capacity or another, found their way into the town. In the earlier years of Madras a single mosque sufficed for all the few Mohammedans therein. The mosque was located in 'Moors Street' in old Black Town, a street that was the predecessor of the 'Moor Street' of to-day. It was not till nearly fifty years after the acquisition of the site of Madras that a second mosque was built—in Muthialpet;

and these two small mosques supplied Mohammedan requirements for many years. The fact is that Madras was so frequently troubled by successive Mohammedan enemies—the King of Golconda; Da-ud Khan, Nawab of the Carnatic; Haidar Ali, Sultan of Mysore; his son Tipu, and others—that the Company was disposed to regard all 'Moors' with mistrust, so much so that they discouraged Mohammedan residents; and a measure was passed with the special intention 'to prevent the Moors purchasing too much land in the Black Town.' There are large crowds of Mohammedans in Madras now, grouped especially in Chepauk and the adjoining Triplicane and Royapettah; and this is due to the fact that in later days Nawab Walajah of Arcot, who was friendly to the English, came and settled down in Madras. He built Chepauk Palace for his residence, and the many Mohammedans who followed him into the city formed the nucleus of a large Mohammedan colony.

The name 'China Bazaar' appears early in the Madras Records; and it would seem to have been the place where Chinese crockery was on sale. Whether or not the salesmen were Chinese immigrants I cannot say; but the fact that another street in Madras bears the name of 'Chinaman Street' suggests that there was at one time a colony of pig-tailed yellow-men in the city. The supposition is not unlikely, for China was included within the sphere of the Company's commercial operations, with Madras as the head-quarters of the trade, and ships of the Company plied regularly between China and Madras. Tea was one of the articles of trade, but Chinese crockery was in great demand in India, and ship-loads of cheap China bowls and plates and dishes were imported; and valuable specimens of Chinese porcelain were highly esteemed by wealthy Indians—so much so that it is on record that one of the Moghul emperors had a slave put to death for having accidentally broken a costly China dish which the emperor particularly admired.

As the Company's trade was very largely in cloth, it can be understood that the Company's agents were eager to induce spinners and weavers to settle in Madras, so that cloth might be bought for the Company at the lowest possible prices from the weavers direct. Elihu Yale, who was one of the early Governors of the Fort, imported some fifty weaver-families and located them in 'Weavers' street', the street that is now known as Nyniappa Naick Street, in Georgetown. Some twenty-five years later, Governor Collet established a number of imported weavers in the northern suburb of Tiruvattur, in a village that was given the name 'Collet Petta' in the Governor's honour—a name that degenerated into 'Kalati Pettah'—'Loafer-land'—its present appellation. There was still a demand for more weavers, and eventually a large vacant tract was marked out as a 'Weavers' Town,' under the name of Chindadre Pettah—the modern Chintadripet. In order to attract weavers, houses were built at the Company's expense, which weavers were permitted to occupy as hereditary possessions. It was formally decreed that "None but Weavers, Spinners, and other persons useful in the Weaving trade, Painters (i.e. designers of patterns for chintz), Washers (bleachers), Dyers, Bettleca-merchants (beetle-sellers), Brahmins and Dancing women, and other necessary attendants on the pagoda (erected in the settlement) shall inhabit the said town." In Chintadripet to-day there are still many spinners and weavers; and one of the sights in Chintadripet—growing gradually more rare—is the spectacle of primitively-clad urchins or grown men spinning in the streets with primitive gear and in primitive fashion; and it is interesting to recall the fact that this has been going on in Chintadripet for nearly two centuries—an industry which the Company established.

Washermanpet is another such locality. It was not so called, as many people imagine, for being a land of dhobies (male laundresses). In the Company's vocabulary a 'washerman' was a man who 'bleached' new-made cloth; and the Company employed a number of bleachers. The bleaching process needed large open spaces—washing-greens—on which the cloth could be laid out in the sun to be bleached; and Washermanpet covered a considerable area.

A great many more of the streets and districts of Madras have history in their names; but the few that we have dealt with suffice to exemplify the manner of the expansion of the city of Madras. We can picture the rustic suppliers crowding into the city to sell the produce of their fields; we can picture the humble weavers migrating into the city with their wives and their children, and with their pots and their pans and their quaint machines, in response to the Company's tempting invitation; we can picture the small tradesmen and the small mechanics setting up their humble shops in the new city in which they believed that fortunes were to be made. And in the higher grades of life we can picture the grave Armenian merchants, the submissive Jews, the mistrusted 'Moors,' and others seeking interviews with Stuart or Georgian-garbed factors of the Company, and eager all of them to turn the Company to profitable account.

CHAPTER V

'THE WALL'

Skirting a thoroughfare in Old Jail Street, in North Georgetown, is still to be seen a part of 'the Wall' that protected Black Town in bygone days. This interesting remnant of the Wall of Madras might before long have been levelled to the ground, either by successive monsoons or by philistine contractors in want of 'material;' but, with a happy regard for a relic of Old Madras, the Madras Government have recently undertaken the task of preserving the ruin, which they have officially declared an 'historic memorial.'

The 'Wall of Madras' is worthy of a meditative visit, but, in order that the meditation may be on an historic basis, it is necessary to know something about the Wall itself.

We have seen that when the Company established themselves at Madras, in 1639, they first built a small fort for the protection of themselves and their goods. Around the walls of the Fort a number of Christians—English and Portuguese and Eurasians—settled down, and what was called 'White Town' came into being. Within a term of years this White Town was itself enclosed within fortified walls, which were finally identical with the wall round Fort St. George to-day. There was thus 'a fort within a fort;' but in course of time the inner wall was pulled down.

Immediately outside the northern wall of White Town lay Black Town, inhabited by Indians—employees and purveyors of the Company, as well as merchants, shopkeepers, industrialists, and the rest. It should be borne in mind that the site of this original Black Town was altogether different from the site of the later Black Town, the 'Georgetown' of to-day. Old Black Town, as already explained, extended from the northern wall of the Fort to what is now called the Esplanade Road, and it covered the ground that is now taken up by the Wireless Telegraph enclosure, the grounds of the High Court, and those of the Law College (*vide* map, p. 10)

Black Town was at first without any wall, and, as the times were unsettled, the place was exposed to the serious

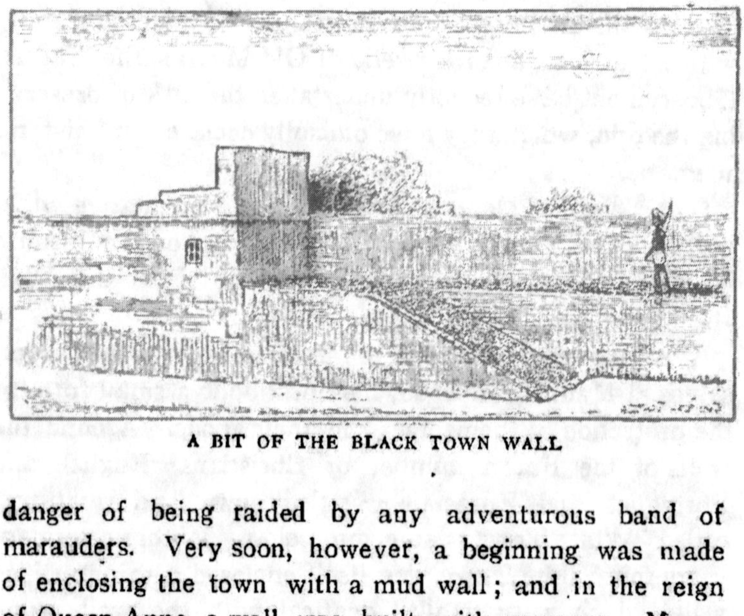

A BIT OF THE BLACK TOWN WALL

danger of being raided by any adventurous band of marauders. Very soon, however, a beginning was made of enclosing the town with a mud wall; and in the reign of Queen Anne a wall was built with masonry. Meanwhile, moreover, numerous houses and streets had sprung up outside the wall, on the site of the Georgetown of to-day.

In 1746 the French captured Fort St. George; and they destroyed not only the Black Town Wall but also Black Town itself. It was a disastrous episode in the history of Madras. For six years the English and the

French had been at war in Europe, and the relations between the English and French colonists in India were naturally strained; but they were settlers within the dominions of Indian rulers, and, although both the English and the French had ships and soldiers for the protection of their settlements, they realized that they were not at liberty to make war upon each other. The settlers, moreover, were employees of mercantile companies, working for dividends; and war, with its calamitous expenditure, was not within their design. But Dupleix, the talented French Governor of Pondicherry, had ambitious ideas for the extension of French influence in India, and, in defiance of Indian rulers, war broke out. In the beginning there were several engagements at sea between a French squadron under Labourdonnais and an English squadron under Captain Peyton. The English squadron was worsted, and had to put into Trincomalee Harbour, in Ceylon, to refit. Thereupon Labourdonnais, after making quick preparations at Pondicherry, sailed for Madras; and the alarm in the Fort and in the city must have been great when his ships appeared off the coast and proceeded to bombard the settlement. His guns, however, did but little damage, and the citizens woke up the next morning to find, to their great content, that the enemy had sailed away during the night. Meanwhile Captain Peyton, having repaired his ships, was unaware of what had happened at Madras, and sailed from Ceylon to Bengal, without touching at Fort St. George. Possibly he was lured to Bengal by bogus messages of French origin; for, as soon as he was out of the way, Labourdonnais reappeared off Madras, better prepared than before. Having succeeded in landing a considerable force, he erected batteries on shore and from various points he bombarded White Town, which was now the actual Fort St. George. At the end of an unhappy seven days the garrison capitulated. The French marched into the Fort, and all the English residents, civil and military—including the Governor and the Members of Council, and also Robert Clive, who was then a young clerk—were sent to Pondicherry as prisoners of war.

For nearly three years the French flag flew over Fort St. George, until, in accordance with the Treaty of

CENTRAL GATE OF THE BLACK TOWN WALL

Aix-la-Chapelle, made between the combatants in Europe, Madras was restored to the Company.

During their occupation the French had made great changes. Feeling the necessity of strengthening their position, their military commanders realized what had apparently not been recognized by the Company's employees, untrained in war—namely that a weak-walled native town lying right against the northern wall of Fort

St. George was a serious danger. The houses offered convenient cover for any enemies that might attack the Fort; and, moreover, any disaffected or venal townsman was in a position to give the assailants valuable help. The French Governor set himself, therefore, to the deliberate destruction of Black Town. He first destroyed the Town Wall, and then—for a distance of 400 yards from the northern wall of White Town, or the present Fort St. George—he demolished every house. The area that is now represented by the Wireless Telegraph Station and the grounds of the High Court thus became an open space. Meanwhile they constructed a moat and glacis round the walls of White Town, which, with certain alterations, are the moat and glacis of Fort St. George to-day.

The Records express the melancholy interest with which the Company's employees, when they re-entered Madras, took note of the changes that the enemy had made in the familiar settlement. The Councillors apparently conceived that it was in a wanton spirit of destruction that the greater part of Black Town had been wiped out; for they formally decided that the streets that had been destroyed should be rebuilt. It may be supposed however, that their military advisers counselled them otherwise; for, so far from the old houses being rebuilt, those that had been left standing were destroyed. The open space was allowed to remain; and 'New Black Town'—the modern 'Georgetown'—began to be developed. It continued to be called 'Black Town' until the visit of the Prince of Wales (afterwards King George V) to Madras in 1906 when it was formally re-named 'Georgetown'—ostensibly in Prince George's honour, but in reality to meet the wishes of a number of the residents who sought an opportunity of getting rid of what they regarded—quite reasonably—as an objectionable name for the locality in which their lot was cast. The disappearance of the historic name is a matter for historic regret, but a concession had to be made to the intelligible wishes of residents.

The Company, bearing in mind that the French had been able to capture Madras, realized that it was necessary to strengthen the defences of Fort St. George and also to provide adequate protection for the new native city that had grown up outside the Fort's protective walls and was absolutely without defence. The defences of the Fort

A MAGAZINE IN THE BLACK TOWN WALL

were taken in hand at once, though the work was by no means completed; and the Directors in England readily sanctioned the construction of a wall round New Black Town. It was well that the security of the Fort was looked to without any long delay; for in 1758, a large French army under Count Lally besieged the Fort again—but so unsuccessfully that, after sixty-seven days of persistent endeavour, they beat a sudden retreat. It was a good many years, however, before the building of the wall round Black Town was taken seriously in hand—and then only because the Company had been given a succession of sharp warnings that it was absolutely necessary that new Black Town should be protected.

The French themselves had given the first warning during the siege under Count Lally; for, although they were powerless against the Fort, they were able to enter Black Town without opposition, and they made use of some of the houses for the purpose of the siege. The next warning was given a few years later when Tipu, the son of Haidar Ali, Sultan of Mysore, after ravaging the country round Madras, came so near to the city itself that parties of his horsemen were scampering about in the suburb of Chintadripet. Tipu's raid induced the Company to bring forth the approved but long-shelved plans for a wall round Black Town; but there was still much more discussion than work. The Company needed yet another awakening; and they got a stern one two years later. We quote the story from the Company's official records, published by the Madras Government. It is contained in a minute in the official Diary of Fort St. George, dated the 29th of March, 1769, which runs as follows :—

> About 8 o'Clock this morning several Parties of the Enemy's (Haidar Ali's) horse appeared in the Bounds of this Place at St. Thomé and Egmore, from which latter place some guns were fired at them. . . . At eleven o'Clock a fellow was caught plundering at Triplicane and brought into Town, who gave Intelligence that Hyder himself was on the other side of St. Thomé with the greatest part of his horse. In the afternoon Advice came that the Enemy's horse were moving from St. Thomé round to the Northward with a design, as was supposed, to make an attempt on the Black Town.

It would have been difficult to have defended the unwalled town; and on the following day the Council of Fort St. George sent Mr. DuPre, Chief Councillor and succeeding Governor, to Haidar Ali's camp, on the other side of the Marmalong Bridge, to come to terms with the invader ; and within three days a treaty had been made. The treaty, said Mr. DuPre, writing to a friend, " will do us no honor : yet it was necessary, and there was no alternative but that or worse."

After this humiliation the building of the Wall was regarded as a pressing necessity ; and within a year the work was practically finished.

'THE OLD AND THE NEW'
Corner of the Medical School built into a portion of the Black Town Wall.

It was well indeed that the work was done ; for a few years afterwards, on the 10th of August, 1780, Haidar's cavalry raided San Thomé and Triplicane, killing a number of people ; and the terror in Black Town was so great that crowds of the inhabitants took flight. Fortunately, however, the Governor was able to issue the following notification for the reassurance of the public :—' A sufficient number of guns have been mounted on the Black Town wall,' and ' nothing has been omitted that I can think of for the security of the Black Town.' Haidar was not sufficiently venturesome to attack the fortified town; but the terror of the inhabitants was by no means at an end; for a little later came the disastrous news that a British force sent out to meet the invader had been cut to pieces at Conjeevaram. Eventually, however, the Mysoreans were defeated, and the treaty of peace was a triumph for the Company.

The long delay in the building of the Wall was chiefly due to the fact that the representatives of the Company, being commercial men, naturally gave their chief attention to the Company's mercantile business, and were apt to disregard the immediate necessity of expensive schemes which the Company's military officers put forward as strategic requirements. When the Wall was first talked about, after the recovery of Madras from the French, the Directors in England, who always kept a tight hand on the Company's purse-strings, declared that the inhabitants of Black Town ought to be made to pay for the cost of their own defences, and should be taxed accordingly; and the name of the 'Wall Tax Road,' which runs alongside the Central Station to the Salt Cotaurs, is a standing reminder of the Directors' decree, while the road itself is an indication of the alignment of the western wall. The people protested indignantly against being taxed for the purpose, and, as a matter of fact, the representatives of the Company in India doubted whether they would be within their legal rights in compelling them to pay; and the tax was never actually levied. What with the Wall Tax Road on the west and the seashore on the east, the existing remains on the north, and the Esplanade on the south, it is not difficult to form a general idea of the direction of the four sides of the wall within which the later Black Town was enclosed.

Such is the story of 'The Wall;' and the remains are an interesting relic of lawless times when at any minute it was possible that crowds of terror-stricken folk would suddenly be pouring through the gateways of the city at the alarming news that strange horsemen were dashing here and there in one or another of the suburbs, demanding money and jewels from the people and slaughtering unhappy individuals who tried to evade a response.

CHAPTER VI

EXPANSION

We have seen that the Company were careful to develop both White Town and Black Town. They were not content, however, with mere developments, for they took pains also to extend their territorial possessions.

The strip of land that was acquired by Mr. Francis Day was not large. Roughly, it extended along the seashore from the mouth of the Cooum to an undefined point beyond the present harbour, somewhere in the neighbourhood of Cassimode, and inland as far as what was called the North River, which is now represented by Cochrane's Canal—the canal that runs between the Central Station and the People's Park. It will be interesting to note how some of the various other parts of the present city came into the Company's possession.

On several occasions the representatives of various dynasties that were successively supreme over Madras made grants of additional land to the Company. The village of Triplicane was the first addition,——some twenty years after the acquisition of Madras. The village was granted by the representative of the Mohammedan King of Golconda, for an annual rent of Rs. 175, which ceased to be paid when the Golconda dynasty shortly afterwards came to an end. Later, in compliance with a petition by Governor Elihu Yale to the Emperor Aurangzeb, the Company received a free grant of 'Tandore (Tondiarpet), Persewacca (Pursewaukam), and Yegmore (Egmore).' Still later, in the reign of Aurangzeb's son and successor, the village

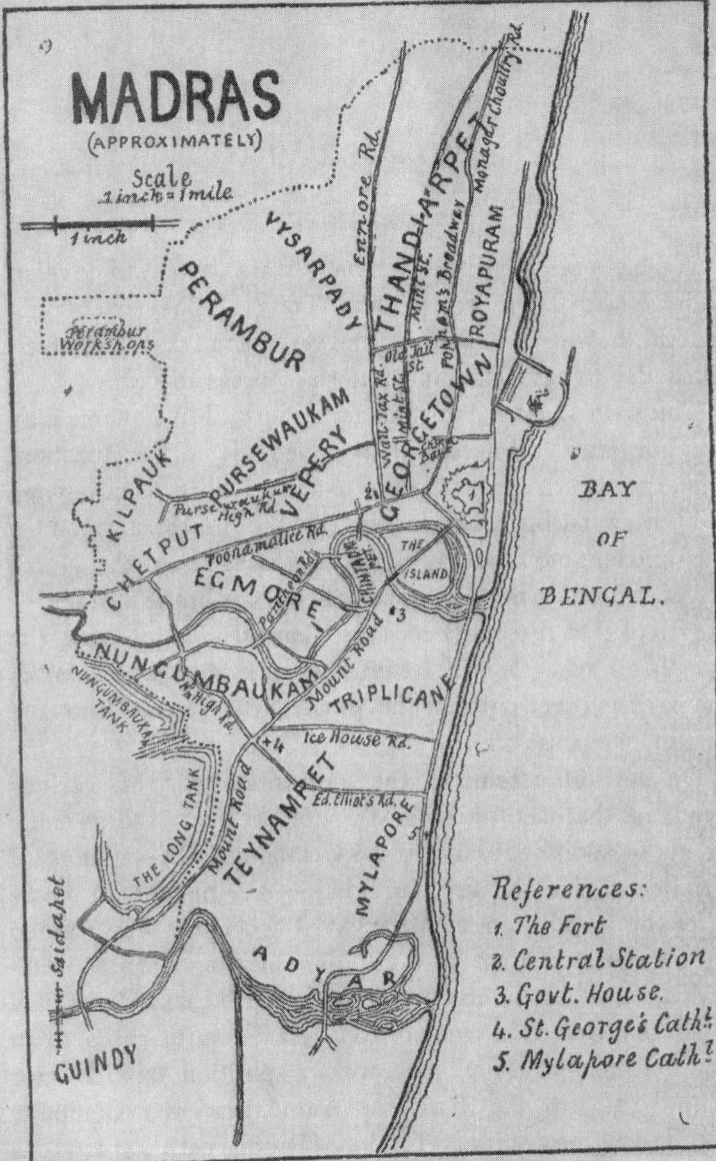
MADRAS
(APPROXIMATELY)
Scale
1 inch = 1 mile
1 inch
PERAMBUR
Perambur Workshops
VYSARPADY
Ennore Rd.
THANDIARPET
Manager Choultry Rd.
Mint St.
Ponnam's Broadway
ROYAPURAM
Old Jail St.
Wall Tax Rd.
GEORGETOWN
PURSEWAUKAM
Pursewaukum High Rd.
VEPERY
KILPAUK
CHETPUT
Poonamallee Rd.
EGMORE
THE ISLAND
NUNGUMBAUKAM
NUNGUMBAUKAM TANK
Mount Road
TRIPLICANE
Ice House Rd.
TEYNAMPET
Ed. Elliot's Rd.
THE LONG TANK
MYLAPORE
ADYAR
Saidapet
GUINDY
BAY OF BENGAL.
References:
1. The Fort
2. Central Station
3. Govt. House.
4. St. George's Cathl.
5. Mylapore Cathl.

of Lungambacca (Nungumbaukam), now the principal residential district of Europeans in Madras, was granted to the Company, together with four adjoining villages, for a total annual rent of 1,500 pagodas (say Rs. 5,250). The Emperor's officers argued that the rent ought to have been larger, but the Company, conforming to the spirit of corruption that was in fashion, were wily enough to send by a Brahman and a Mohammedan conjointly a sum of Rs. 700 'to be distributed amongst the King's officers who keep the Records, in order to settle this matter.' The village of Vepery—variously called in olden documents Ipere, Ypere, Vipery, and Vapery—lay between Egmore and Pursewaukam; and the Company, being naturally desirous of consolidating their territory, proceeded at once to try to obtain a grant of the place; but successive efforts on the part of Governor Elihu Yale came to naught; and it was not till much later (1742) when the Nawab of Arcot was lord of the soil, that Vepery was acquired from the Nawab. The manner of its acquisition is interesting. The preceding Nawab had just been murdered, and the Carnatic army disowning the ambitious rival who had murdered him, proclaimed the dead Nawab's son as his successor. The new Nawab was but a youth, and he was residing at the time in one of the big houses in Black Town. The Company were politic enough to celebrate the lad's accession with grand doings. They escorted him in a splendid procession to the Company's Gardens, which were situated along the bank of the river Cooum, where the General Hospital and the Medical College now stand. In the Gardens there was a fine house, containing a spacious hall, which the Company had specially designed for great occasions; and there the lad's accession was formally announced; and finally he was escorted in procession back to his dwelling. The Company profited by their politic demonstration; for, in return for their courtesies to the young

Nawab, the lad gratified their desires by making them a rent-free grant of the village of Vepery, and also of Perambore and other lands. It may be added that the boy-king was unfortunate; for he was murdered within two years of his accession, at the instance of the man who had murdered his father.

San Thomé was acquired in 1749; and the story of the acquisition is not without interest. The names 'San Thomé' and 'Mylapore' are often used as alternative designations for one and the same locality; but in bygone days the two names represented quite different places. Mylapore was a very ancient Indian town, which seems to have been in existence long before the birth of Christ. San Thomé was a seventeenth century Portuguese settlement close by. It is an old tradition that St. Thomas the Apostle was martyred just outside Mylapore; and when the Portuguese first came to India some of them visited Mylapore to look for relics of the saint. They found some ruined Christian churches, and also a tomb which they believed to be the tomb of St. Thomas; and soon afterwards a Portuguese monastery was established on the spot. A Portuguese town grew up around the monastery; and in course of time the town became a commercial centre, and was surrounded with a fortified wall, and was the Portuguese settlement of San Thomé, over against the Indian town of Mylapore. An Italian dealer in precious stones who visited India in the sixteenth century wrote of San Thomé that it was 'as fair a city' as any that he had seen in the land; and he described Mylapore as being an Indian city surrounded by its own mud wall. Mylapore was thus in effect the Black Town of San Thomé; but in later days the two towns were combined. When the English came to Fort St. George, the power of the Portuguese was already waning; and the development of the influence of the English at Madras meant a further lessening of the influence of the Portuguese at San Thomé; and it was a natural consequence that San Thomé, including Mylapore, became a prey to possession assailants. Its first captor was the lord of the lord the Mohammedan King of Golconda. Next, the French took it from Golconda; and two years later Golconda, with the help of the Dutch, recaptured it from the French. The Dutch were content with a share of the plunder for their reward, and left Golconda in possession. On the self-interested advice of the English at Fort St. George, Golconda destroyed the fortifications. He then put the town up for sale. The Company were prepared to buy it, and so were the Portuguese; but a rich Mohammedan named Cassa Verona found favour with Golconda's Moslem officials, and secured the town on a short lease. Next it was leased to the Hindu Governor of Poonamallee; and then for a big price it went back again to the Portuguese. Towards the end of the seventeenth century the great Moghul Emperor Aurangzeb dethroned the lord of the soil, the King of Golconda; and, although the Portuguese were not turned out of San Thomé, it was now a part of the Moghul Empire, and was put in charge of a Moslem ruler. After Aurangzeb's death, the Moghul Empire broke up, and the Nawab of Arcot eventually became independent, and San Thomé was part of his dominions. In 1749, when Madras, after the French occupation, was restored to the English by an order from Paris, in accordance with the treaty of Aix la Chapelle, Dupleix at Pondicherry was bitterly disappointed at the rendition, and he formed designs for the acquisition of San Thomé for France, as a set-off for the loss of Madras. The English at Fort St. George had information of his schemes, and, being in no way desirous of having aggressive Frenchmen for close neighbours, they forestalled Dupleix by persuading the Nawab to make the Company a grant of 'Mylapore, *alias* St. Thomé,' on condition that the Company should undertake to help the

Nawab with men and money whenever he should call upon them to do so. It was thus that San Thomé became a British possession ; and, although it was afterwards ravaged successively by the French under Count Lally and by Haidar Ali of Mysore, it has remained a British possession ever since.

We have said enough to show the manner in which the different parts of the modern city of Madras came into the hands of the English. The methods were not always wholly admirable ; but we must remember that the East India Company was a mercantile association, fighting for its existence under diamond-cut-diamond conditions ; and we must remember also that, although its representatives at Madras were sent out to India not to rule but to earn dividends for the shareholders, yet the Company's rule over Madras was so upright that crowds of people were continually flocking into Madras to enjoy its benefits.

CHAPTER VII

OUTPOSTS

The suburban lands which were successively granted to the Company were not protected either by the walls of Fort St. George or by the walls of Black Town, and it was accordingly necessary that special means should be adopted for their defence. The Company's military engineers devised the erection of small suburban forts ('redoubts'), block-houses, and batteries, which were to be mounted with cannon and to be in charge of an appropriate garrison, and were to serve as outposts for the protection of the outlying quarters of the city.

On the northern side of Black Town the batteries and block-houses were linked together by a thick-set hedge of palmyras, bamboos, prickly-pear, and thorny bushes, such that neither infantry nor cavalry could force a way through. Later it was decreed that the 'Bound Hedge,' as it was called, should be extended so as to encircle the whole city. The work, however, was never completed, for as late as 1785 an influential European inhabitant of Madras, addressing the Government on the subject of the insecurity of the city, wrote :—

> "Was the Bound Hedge finished, no man could desert, No Spy could pass ; provisions would be cheap. All the Garden Houses, as well as thirty-three Square Miles of Ground, would be in security from the invasions of irregular Horse."

Of the suburban fortifications the two largest were at Egmore and at San Thomé. Next in size were those at Nungumbaukam and at Pursewaukam. Of smaller works there were many. Of the fortifications at Nungumbaukam

A PORTION OF THE EXTENSIVE RUINS IN THE GROUNDS OF 'LEITH CASTLE,' SAN THOME

and at Pursewaukam all traces have disappeared; but of the larger ones at San Thomé and at Egmore interesting remains are still to be seen.

The remains of the San Thomé Redoubt stand within the grounds of 'Leith Castle,' a house that lies south of the San Thomé Cathedral. The remains are ruins, but the massive walls fifteen feet high and three feet thick, are suggestive of the purpose for which the redoubt was built. The 'Records' show that the San Thomé Redoubt, built in 1751, was a very complete fortification, with a moat forty feet wide, a glacis, and all the other works that are usual in respect of a well appointed building of the kind. That it was of a large size is to be seen in the fact that, when the French under Count Lally were besieging Madras, an English officer was officially directed 'to stay in St. Thomé Fort with the Europeans belonging to Chingleput, four Companies of sepoys, and fifty horse.'

The Egmore Redoubt was a good deal older than that of San Thomé. It was constructed in the days of Queen Anne. It was intended, of course, for the special protection of Egmore; but in those distant days when trips to the hills were unknown, even Egmore was a health-resort in respect of the crowded Fort St. George, and it was officially reported that the Egmore Redoubt might 'serve for a convenience for the sick Soldiers when arrived from England, for the recovery of their health, it being a good air.' The Egmore Redoubt was evidently a need; for the 'Records' tell us that on various occasions its guns were fired at the enemy. The enemy were for the most part horsemen of Haidar Ali or of Tipu, his son and successor; and in 1799 the year in which Tipu was killed, the need for the Redoubt disappeared. Adjoining the precincts of the Redoubt were the premises of the Male Asylum, an Anglo-Indian Orphanage, which required to be extended, and in the following year the Madras

Government gave the Redoubt to the Asylum, and the two premises were turned into a common enclosure. In the beginning of the present century the Directors of the Asylum sold their Egmore estate to the South Indian Railway Company and removed to new premises in the Poonamallee road; and what remains of the Egmore Redoubt is now the habitation of some of the Railway employees.

THE EGMORE FORT (SIDE VIEW)

The remains are of quaint interest. At some date or another the authorities of the Asylum had an upper story added to one of the military buildings, with the result that there is the strange spectacle of a row of windowed chambers on the top of a buttressed and battlemented wall, windowless and grim. The upper story has been built into the battlements in such a manner that the outline of the battlements is still clearly visible, and the building is a composite reminder of old-time war and latter-day peace.

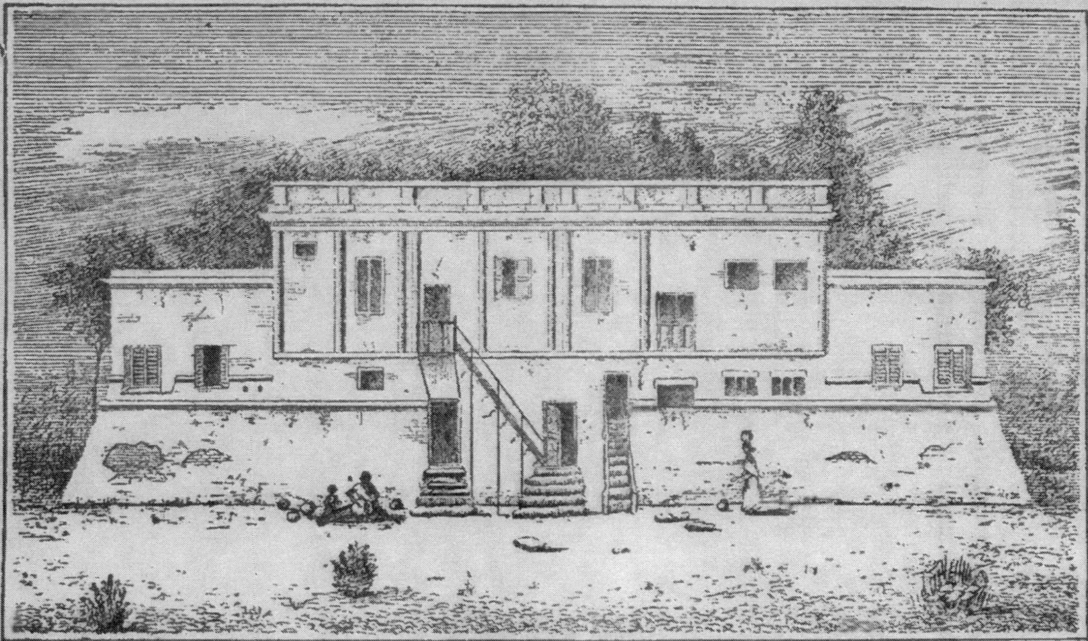

REMAINS OF THE EGMORE FORT.

The building to be the Male Asylum Road, and is now the residence of some railway employees. Its upper part has been built upon a battlemented wall, and doors have been let into the wall. The outlines of the original wall and of some of the battlements can be easily traced.

The whole of the lower part of the building, with its massive walls and its frowning aspect, is of curious and suggestive interest; and the ground around, which is extensively bricked, is a reminder of the fact that the Redoubt in its original form was large indeed. The place provides interesting material for antiquarian speculation.

CHAPTER VIII

THE CHURCH IN THE FORT

St. Mary's Church within the walls of Fort St. George is the oldest Protestant church in India, and, except for some of the oldest bits of the Fort walls, it is the oldest British building in Madras city, and even in India itself. It dates from 1680.

When Madras was rising upon its foundations, the Company's employees were not only without a church but also without a pastor; for the Company did not think it necessary to go to the expense of providing a chaplain for so small a community. But it was an age in which religious services on Sunday were seldom neglected; and it may be conceived that, in default of a chaplain at Fort St. George, the Governor himself or his delegate read the Church Service on Sunday morning and evening, in the hearing of the assembled employees of the Company, and perhaps also some selections from the published sermons of distinguished Elizabethan divines.

In the Portuguese settlement of San Thomé there were numerous Roman Catholic priests, and some of them ministered to the numerous Portuguese and other Roman Catholic residents of White Town around Fort St. George, as also of Black Town close by. So numerous indeed were the Roman Catholic residents of White Town within three years of the foundation of the Fort that the Governor permitted a French priest to build a chapel in the Town. It was thus not a little anomalous that in a British settlement, founded under the auspices of such a redoubted antipapist as Queen Elizabeth, there was a Roman Catholic church with a priest in charge, yet neither a church nor a pastor of the established religion.

In 1645, however, the Company's Agent at Fort St. George forwarded to higher authority "a petition from the souldiers for the desireing of a minister to be here with them for the maintainance of their soules health;" and in the following year a chaplain was sent out. There was still no Protestant church, but the celebration of religious services was held in careful regard; for the chaplain read morning and evening prayers every day of the year in a room in the Fort appointed for the purpose, and it was compulsory upon all the youthful employees of the Company to attend regularly, under the penalty of a fine.

Chaplains came and chaplains went, and for some sixteen years they continued their ministrations in the room in the Fort. A small church was then built; but, with the Company's developing trade, the population of White Town increased so rapidly that before long the little church was too small for the number of the worshippers. When Mr. Streynsham Master, after a long term of years in the Company's service, was appointed Governor of Madras, one of his first acts was the circulation of a voluntary subscription paper for the building of a church that should be worthy of the Company's rapidly developing South Indian possession. He headed the list with a subscription of a hundred pagodas (Rs. 350), a sum which represented much more than it does now; for it was more than Mr. Streynsham Master's pay for a whole month as Governor of Madras. Subscriptions from the Councillors, as well as from the factors and writers and apprentices, were proportionately big; and on the 28th of October, 1680, St. Mary's Church was solemnly opened, and the guns of the Fort roared forth loud volleys in honour of the event. The steeple and the sanctuary were added later; but, for the rest, the present church, except for details, is the very same church that was built some two hundred and fifty years ago, in the reign of Charles II.

It is interesting to note that the church at Madras was built during a period when in London a great many churches were being built—or rebuilt—after the Great Fire. Church-building was in vogue, with the distinguished Sir Christopher Wren as the builder in chief; and it is not unlikely that what was being done so energetically in London was one of the influences that inspired Mr. Streynsham Master to be so earnest over a scheme for building a church in Madras. It may be noted, moreover, that St. Mary's Church within the Fort at Madras is of a style that was very much in fashion in London at the time.

ST. MARY'S, FORT ST. GEORGE.

In deciding to build a new church, the Governor and his colleagues realized that if ever the Fort should be bombarded, a shot from the enemy's guns was as likely to fall upon the church as upon a fortified bastion; so the roof of the church was made 'bomb-proof,' in preparation for possibilities. Events proved the reasonableness of the measure; for on more than one occasion the church was a factor in war.

In 1746, when the French were besieging Fort St. George, the British defenders lodged their wives and children and their domestic servants in the bomb-proof church, and they took refuge there themselves in the intervals of military duty. During the three years that they occupied Madras, the French, fearing that they might be besieged in their turn, used the bomb-proof church as a storehouse for grain and as a reservoir for drinking-water. The church organ they sent off to Pondicherry as one of the spoils of war.

At the end of the war Madras was restored to the Company, but a few years later the Fort was besieged by the French again. During the interval, some of the houses had been made bomb-proof, and in these the women and children were lodged, but St. Mary's Church was used as a barrack, and its steeple as a watch-tower. Lally, the French commander, failing to capture Madras, had to march away with his hopes baffled; but, notwithstanding its bomb-proof roof, the church, as also its steeple, had been badly damaged during the destructive siege, and the necessary repairs were considerable.

A few years later the English had their revenge. They captured Pondicherry, and they destroyed its fortifications. They recovered, with other things, the organ that had been looted from St. Mary's; but, as a new one had in the meanwhile been obtained for St. Mary's, the recovered instrument was sent to a church up-country. According to accounts, moreover, they took toll for the Frenchmen's loot by sending to St. Mary's from one of the churches in Pondicherry the large and well-executed painting of the 'Last Supper,' which is still to be seen in the church. The origin of the picture is not known for certain; but it is believed with reason to be a fact that it was a spoil of war from Pondicherry on one or another of the three occasions on which that town was captured by the British.

The stray visitor who wanders round St. Mary's without a guide is apt to be astonished at what he sees in the churchyard. A multitude of old tombstones, of various ages and with inscriptions in various tongues, lie flat on the ground, as close to one another as paving-stones, in such fashion that the visitor must wonder how there can be sufficient room for coffins below. As a matter of fact, the coffins and their contents are not there, and the inscriptions of 'Here lyeth' and 'Hic jacet' are not statements of facts. The explanation is an interesting story, which is worth the telling.

In the Company's early days, the 'English Burying Place,' (*vide* Map, p. 10) lay a little way outside the walls of White Town, in an area which is now occupied by the Madras Law College with its immediate precincts. Later, when a wall was built round old Black Town, the Burial Ground was included within the enclosure of the wall. An English cemetery in a corner of an Indian town was not likely to be treated with any particular respect; and on various counts the 'English Burying Place' was a sadly neglected spot. Nearly every Englishman that died in Madras was an employee of the Company, and was a bachelor, without any relatives in India to mourn his loss His colleagues gave him a grand funeral; but his death meant promotion for some of those selfsame colleagues, and his place in the Company's service was filled up by an official 'Order' on the following day. A big monument in the old-fashioned brick-and-mortar ugliness was piously built over his remains, and possibly there was genuine regret at a good fellow's loss; but water is less thick than blood, and there was no near one or dear one in India to take affectionate care of the big tomb; so it was left to itself to be taken care of by the people of Black Town. An unofficial description of Madras dated 1711 speaks of the 'stately Tombs' in the English cemetery, and an official Record of the same year speaks of the unhallowed uses to which the stately tombs were put. The Record says that "Excesses are Comitted on hallowed ground," and that the arcaded monuments were "turned into receptacles for Beggars and Buffaloes." We have seen in a previous chapter that the French, when they captured Madras, demolished the greater part of old Black Town together with its wall, and that the English, when they were back in Madras, completed the work of demolition. In the two-fold destruction, both French and English had sufficient respect for the dead to leave the tombs alone. But, now that Black Town was gone, the big tombs were the nearest buildings to the walls of White Town and Fort St. George; and when the French under Lally besieged Madras a few years later, they used the 'stately Tombs' as convenient cover for their attack on the city. The cemetery now was a receptacle not for beggars and buffaloes but for soldiers and guns. The siege lasted sixty-seven days, during which the cemetery was a vantage ground for successive French batteries. It is therefore not to be wondered at that when Count Lally had raised the unsuccessful siege, the authorities at Fort St. George decided that the 'stately tombs' were to disappear. The tombs themselves were accordingly destroyed, but the slabs that bore the inscriptions were laid in St. Mary's churchyard. At a later date some of them were taken up and were removed to the ramparts, for the extraordinary purpose of 'building platforms for the guns,'[1] but eventually they were restored to the churchyard and were relaid as we see them to-day.

When the burying ground was dismantled, two of its monuments were allowed to remain. They are still to be seen on the Esplanade, outside the Law College, and the inscriptions can still be read; and the two tombs are interesting memorials of the past. One is a tall, steeple-like structure, which represents a woman's grief for her first husband, and for her child by her second. Her first husband was Joseph Hynmers, Senior Member of Council, who died in 1680, her second was Elihu Yale, Governor of Madras, whom she married six months after the death of her first. When her little son David died at the age of four, she had him buried in her first husband's grave. The other monument covers a vault which holds the remains of various members of the Powney family, a name which figured freely in the list of the Company's employees throughout the eighteenth century. When the cemetery was dismantled, members of the Powney family were still in the Madras service, and it was doubtless in respect for their feelings that the vault was not disturbed.

It may be added that amongst the gravestones that pave the ground outside St. Mary's Church there are several that record the death of Roman Catholics. It is supposed that they were taken from the graveyard of the Roman Catholic church in White Town, which was demolished by the Company when they recovered Madras after the French occupation.

Although the gravestones around St. Mary's Church bear the names of persons who were buried elsewhere, there are memorials within the church itself which mark the actual resting-place of mortal remains. Most of the

[1] Rev. F. Penny's *Church in Madras*, vol. i, p. 366.

monuments in St. Mary's are of historic interest, and it is fascinating indeed to stroll round the building and study

Storied urn or animated bust;

but it is noteworthy that no inscription records the very first burial within the walls of the church. It is noteworthy too that the forgotten grave was not the grave of an obscure person, but of Lord Pigot, Governor of Madras; and, in view of the extraordinary circumstances of his death, the first burial is the most notable of all.

George Pigot was sent out to Madras as a lad of eighteen, to take up the post of a writer in the Company's service. He worked so well that he rose rapidly, and at the early age of thirty-six he was appointed Governor of Madras. It was in the middle of his eight years' governorship that the French under Lally besieged Madras for sixty-five days; and Governor Pigot's untiring energy and skilful measures were prime factors in the successful defence. After the war he did great things for the development of Madras; and when he resigned office at the age of forty-five and went to England, the strenuous upholder of British honour in the East was rewarded with an Irish peerage. Well would it have been for Lord Pigot if he had settled down for good on his Irish estate! But twelve years later he accepted the offer of a second term of office as Governor of Madras. It is not infrequently the case that a man who has been eminently successful in office at one time of his career fails badly if after a long interval he accepts the same office again. Times have altered and methods that were successful before are now out of date. In Lord Pigot's case the conditions at the time of his second appointment were very different from those at the time of the first. On the first occasion he had risen to office with colleagues who had been his companions in the service. On the second occasion he was sent out to Madras as an elderly nobleman selected for the job, and as a stranger to his colleagues, who moreover were particularly given to factious disputes. It is not unlikely too that Lord Pigot himself had become touchy and overbearing in his declining years. Any way, he quarrelled with his Councillors almost immediately, and within six or seven months there had been some very angry scenes. He had been accustomed to being obeyed, and in his wrath at being obstinately resisted he went to the length of ordering the arrest not only of some of the leading members of Council but also of the Commander-in-Chief. The Councillors check-mated the Governor's order by arresting the Governor! It was a daring proceeding. He was arrested one night after dark, while driving along a suburban road on his imagined way to a friendly supper, and he was sent as a prisoner to a house at St. Thomas's Mount. He was in captivity for some nine months, while the triumphant Councillors were representing their case to the Directors in England; and then he died, in Government House, Madras, to which when he fell ill he had been transferred. It is on record that his remains were specially honoured with burial within St. Mary's Church—the first burial within the building—but no permanent memorial was raised to the unhappy Governor's memory; and the particular spot where he was buried is only a matter of conjecture.

St. Mary's Church is less than 250 years old. Compared with hundreds of the grey-walled or ivy-covered churches in England, St. Mary's at Madras is prosaically new; but it is of exceeding interest nevertheless. Madras itself is a great and historic city, which owes its existence to British enterprise, with Indian co-operation, and St. Mary's Church, as the oldest British building therein, is the earliest milestone of progress. It is not a church that is best visited, like Melrose Abbey, 'in the pale moonlight,' but in the bright daylight, when the inscriptions on the tombstones without and on the monuments within can be clearly read.

CHAPTER IX

ROMAN CATHOLIC, MADRAS

When the English first came to Madras, there were numerous Roman Catholic churches in the neighbouring Portuguese settlement of San Thomé, but there were none within the tract of land that Mr. Francis Day acquired in the Company's behalf. When, therefore, at the Company's invitation, a number of Portuguese from San Thomé, both pure-blooded and mixed, came and settled down in the Company's White Town, they were necessarily compelled to resort to the ministrations of Portuguese priests who belonged to the San Thomé Mission; and within a year of the foundation of Fort St. George, the Portuguese missionaries built a church in the outskirts of the British settlement. This was the Church of the Assumption, which stands in what is still called 'Portuguese Street' in Georgetown, and is therefore a building of historic note. To the Company's representatives the ministrations of Portuguese priests to residents of Madras were objectionable; for the relations between Madras and San Thomé were by no means friendly. It is true that when Mr. Francis Day was treating for the acquisition of a site, the Portuguese at Mylapore had furthered his efforts; but such a mark of apparent good will was no more than the outcome of Portuguese hostility to the Dutch; for they hoped that the English at Madras would be powerful allies with themselves against the aggressive Hollanders. As soon, however, as Madras had begun to be built and English trade to be actively pushed, jealousies arose and disagreements occurred; and the Company's representatives chafed at the idea that Portuguese priests should be the spiritual advisers of residents of Madras.

In 1642, when Madras was in its third year, a certain Father Ephraim, a French Capuchin, chanced to set foot in Madras. Father Ephraim had been sent out from Paris as a missionary to Pegu; and he had travelled across India from Surat to Masulipatam, where, according to his instructions, he was to have secured a passage to Pegu in one of the Company's ships. His information was out of date; for the Agency had lately been transferred from Masulipatam to Madras, and the Company's ships for Pegu were sailing now from Madras instead of from Masulipatam; so Father Ephraim journeyed southward from Masulipatam to look for a vessel at the new settlement. At Madras no vessel was starting immediately, and Father Ephraim had to bide his time. Meanwhile he made himself useful by ministering to the Roman Catholics of the place. Official and other documents show that Father Ephraim was a very devout and a very able man. He was 'an earnest Christian,' 'a polished linguist,' able to converse in English, Portuguese and Dutch, besides his own French, and he was conversant with Persian and Arabic. He had the charm of attractive friendliness, which is so common with Frenchmen, and he captivated all with whom he conversed. The Portuguese and other Roman Catholic inhabitants of Madras, to whom the Company's disapproval of the ministrations of Portuguese priests had been a frequent source of trouble, formally petitioned Father Ephraim to settle down in the city; and the Governor in Council, greatly preferring a French priest to a Portuguese and thoroughly approving of Father Ephraim personally, supported the petition with a formal order that, if the priest would stay, a site would be provided on which he might build a church for his flock. Father Ephraim himself was not unwilling to stay, but he was under orders for Pegu, and, furthermore, Madras was within the diocese of San Thomé, and the Bishop was not likely to approve of a scheme in which the ministrations of his own priests would be set at naught in favour of a stranger. The Company, however, was influential. A reference was made to Father Ephraim's Capuchin superiors in Paris, and they approved of his remaining in Madras; another reference was made to Rome, asking that the British territory of Madras should be ecclesiastically separated from the Portuguese diocese of Mylapore, and the Pope issued a decree to that effect.

A site for a church, as also for a priest's house, was provided in White Town, within the Fort St. George of to-day, and a small church, dedicated to St. Andrew, was built; and for a good many years it was the only church of any kind in the settlement.

The Portuguese ecclesiastics of Mylapore were never reconciled to this ecclesiastical separation of Madras, and when Father Ephraim went by invitation to Mylapore to discuss certain ecclesiastical business, he was forthwith arrested, clapped in irons, and shipped off to Goa and lodged in the prison of the Inquisition. The Governor of Fort St. George took the matter in hand, but Father Ephraim was in prison more than two years before he was eventually released and sent back to Madras.

Later, Father Ephraim rebuilt St. Andrew's Church on a larger plan, and the building was opened with ceremony; and Master Patrick Warner, the Company's Protestant Chaplain at Fort St. George, complained indignantly to the Directors in England that Governor Langhorn had celebrated the popish occasion with the 'firing of great guns' and with 'volleys' of small shot by all the soldiers in garrison.'

Father Ephraim had already built a church in old Black Town, which seems to have stood somewhere within what is now the site of the High Court. Another French

Capuchin had meanwhile come to Madras to help him in his ministrations to his ever-increasing flock; so the church in Black Town had its regular pastor.

After more than fifty years of self-sacrificing work in Madras, Father Ephraim died of old age, sincerely esteemed by all who knew him.

Some years after his death St. Andrew's was again rebuilt, and it was now a large edifice, with a high bell-tower, and a small churchyard around. In the suburban district of Muthialpet there was also a 'Portuguese Burying Place,' which is now the 'compound' of the Roman Catholic Cathedral and its associated buildings in Armenian Street; and a small church stood within this enclosure. Adjoining the Portuguese Burying Place was the 'Armenian Burying Place,' which is now the enclosure of the Armenian church; and it was the Armenian Burying Place that gave the name to the street.

When Madras was captured by the French, there were people who said that the French priests in Madras had given information to their countrymen; and three years later, when Madras was restored to the Company, the Governor in Council confiscated St. Andrew's church. A reference to the Directors in England as to what they were to do with the confiscated building brought back the very decisive reply that they were "immediately on the receipt of this, without fail to demolish the Portuguese Church in the White Town at Madras, and not suffer it to stand." The church was demolished accordingly, as also a Roman Catholic chapel in Vepery. The church in old Black Town had already been demolished by the French when they destroyed the greater part of old Black Town itself; and, in accordance with another edict of the Directors in England, by which the Company's representatives in Madras were "absolutely forbid suffering any Romish Church within the bounds, or even to suffer the public profession of the Romish religion," Roman Catholicism was altogether scouted in Madras.

Twenty-five years later, the English troops, after defeating the French in various engagements, captured Pondicherry and demolished its fortifications; and the peace of Paris left the French in India powerless. With the danger of French aggression removed for good, the Company were less intolerant of the religion which Frenchmen professed; and a few years later they paid the Capuchin priests some Rs. 50,000 as compensation for the destruction of the church in White Town and of the chapel in Vepery.

With funds thus in their hands, the Capuchin fathers set about building a new church in the 'Burying Place.' This new church, which they built in 1775, was the edifice which is now the Roman Catholic Cathedral in Armenian Street. On the gate-posts appears the date 1642, but this was the year in which the Company made a grant of the land for a Roman Catholic Cemetery and in which Father Ephraim arrived and the Madras Mission began, and is not the date of the building of the present church or of its predecessor. The Capuchin missionaries continued in charge of Roman Catholic affairs in Madras until 1832, in which year they were put under episcopal jurisdiction.

Reference has been made in this chapter and elsewhere to the churches that were already in existence in Mylapore when the English first settled in Madras. According to local tradition, the Apostle St. Thomas made his way to the East, and, after preaching in various parts of India, settled down in the ancient Hindu town of Mylapore, where he made numerous converts. The Hindu priests, indignant at the loss of so many of their clients, sought the missionary's life. The Apostle, according to the tradition, lived in a small cave on a small hill—the 'Little Mount'—fed by birds and drinking the water of a spring that bubbled up miraculously within the cave. Driven from the cave, he fled to another hill, a mile or so away—'St. Thomas's Mount'—where he was killed with a lance. The dead body was buried at Mylapore. Such is the story; and in the present-day church on the Little Mount the visitor is shown a cave which is said to have been the Apostle's hiding-place; and within the nave of the cathedral at Mylapore he is shown a hole in the ground—now lined with marble—in which the Martyr's remains are said to have been buried.

When the Portuguese came to Mylapore in the early part of the sixteenth century, they built a church upon the ruins of an ancient church that had enclosed the tomb; and the new church became eventually the Cathedral of San Thomé. The sixteenth century building was pulled down in 1893, and the present Cathedral—a handsome Gothic structure—was built. Mylapore is now a suburb of Madras, and is within British dominion; but the bishopric, which was originally supported by the King of Portugal, who had the right of nominating the bishop, is still supported by the Portuguese Government.

Mylapore has a history of its own that is outside the scope of the 'Story of Madras;' but a few words about the glories of a city that is now a suburb of Madras will not be out of place.

Mylapore and Madras, standing side by side, are a conjunction of the old and the young. Mylapore, or Meliapore, the 'Peacock City' of the ancient Hindu world, has existed for twenty centuries, and perhaps a great many more; Madras has existed less than three. It was at Mylapore that, according to tradition, the body of the martyred Apostle St. Thomas was buried; Mylapore was the birth-place of Tiruvalluvar, an old and illustrious Tamil author who belonged to the down-trodden class, and of Peyalvar, an eminent Vaishnavite saint and writer; it was here that a company of Saivaite saints, Appar and his fellows, assembled together and wrote their well-known hymns; and it was here also that Mastan, a renowned Mohammedan scholar, lived and wrote and died.

Of the ancient glories of Mylapore no vestige remains; but several of the churches of the Mylapore diocese belong to the sixteenth century, including the celebrated 'Luz' Church, the Church of the Madre-de-Deus at San Thomé and the little Church of Our Lady of Refuge between Mylapore and Saidapet, besides the churches at the Little Mount and St. Thomas's Mount, of which the latter is a sixteenth-century development of an old chapel that existed there before the coming of the Portuguese.

It is of interest to note that there are those who say that a Mylapore church gave its name to the city of Madras. They say—not, I believe, without evidence—that the rural village of Madraspatam, where Mr. Francis Day selected a site for the Company's settlement, had been colonized by fisherfolk from the parish of the Madre-de-Deus Church—the Church of the Mother of God—and that the emigrant fisherfolk called their village by the name of their parish, and that the name was eventually corrupted into 'Madras.' The origin of the name 'Madras' is uncertain; and the explanation is at any rate interesting and not unlikely to be true.

CHAPTER X

CHEPAUK PALACE

Among the interesting buildings in Madras must be included Chepauk Palace, which was built about a century and a half ago as a residence for the Nawab of the Carnatic, and which is now the office of the Board of Revenue. The high wall that enclosed the spacious Saracenic structure in its palace days has been pulled down, and the public can now gaze at a building that was once carefully screened from the public eye, and can enter at will without having to satisfy the scrutiny of armed men at the gate. A change indeed—from the sleepy residence of a Muhammadan ruler, with his harem and his idle crowd of retainers, to bustling offices where a multitude of officials and clerks are working out the cash accounts of the Government of Madras!

The 'Carnatic' was a dominion that extended over the territory that is now included in the Collectorates of Nellore, North Arcot, South Arcot, Trichinopoly, and Tinnevelly. The town of Arcot was the capital of the dominion, and the Nawab of the Carnatic was sometimes spoken of as the Nawab of Arcot. Chepauk Palace belongs to the history of the Carnatic, and a few historical notes will make things clear.

In our first chapter we intimated that Madras, when Mr. Francis Day acquired it, was within the domain of the disappearing Hindu Empire of Vijianagar, of which the living representative at the time was the Raja of Chandragiri, from whom Mr. Francis Day accordingly obtained a deed of possession. Seven years afterwards, the Raja of Chandragiri was a refugee in Mysore, driven from his throne by the Muhammadan Sultan of Golconda, who assumed the sovereignty of Hyderabad and the Carnatic. The Sultan of Golconda thus became the recognized overlord of Madras; and the Company were careful to secure from their new sovereign a confirmation of their possession. But the power of the Sultan was destined to fall in its turn; for Aurangzeb, the Moghul Emperor at Delhi, being desirous of uniting all India under Moghul rule, waged war against the Sultan of Golconda—who, as a Shiah Mohammedan, was a heretic in Aurangzeb's eyes—and defeated him. Aurangzeb put Hyderabad under a Nizam whom he named 'Viceroy of the Deccan' and the Carnatic under a Nawab who was to be subordinate to the Viceroy. But the Emperor who succeeded Aurangzeb had none of their predecessors' greatness; and soon after Aurangzeb's death the Nizam of Hyderabad assumed independence, with the Nawab of the Carnatic as his vassal.

In 1749 there was a quarrel for the Nawabship. The French at Pondicherry supported one claimant, and the English at Madras supported the other. This was the gallant Clive's opportunity. Exchanging the clerk's pen for the officer's sword, the youthful 'writer' marched with a small force to Arcot and captured it on behalf of the Company's nominée, and then sustained most heroically a lengthy siege. Clive triumphed; and Mohammed Ali, otherwise known as Nawab Walajah, became undisputed Nawab of the Carnatic. Later, with British support, the Nawab renounced his allegiance to Hyderabad, and reigned as an independent prince.

In his capital at Arcot, Nawab Walajah, who had many factionary enemies, would assuredly have found himself in a dangerous centre of intrigue; but he was wise in his generation; for as soon as he had gained his independence he sought and obtained from the Governor of Madras permission to build a palace for himself within the protective walls of Fort St. George. Arrangements for the work were made; and one of the streets of the Fort—the street which still bears the name of 'Palace Street'—received its name because it was the street in which the Nawab's residence was to be built. Eventually, however, the scheme was set aside; and in the following year the Nawab acquired private property in Chepauk, and engaged an English architect to build him a house. Chepauk Palace thus came into existence. The grounds of the Palace, which the Nawab surrounded with a wall, formed an immense enclosure, which included a large part of the grounds of Government House of today and a great deal of adjoining land.

Chepauk Palace was the scene of some grand doings in its time; and soon after it was built the Nawab entertained the Governor of Madras and his Councillors, one of whom was Mr. Warren Hastings, at 'an elegant breakfast;' and, when the feast was over, he divided some Rs. 30,000 among his guests. The Governor got Rs. 7,000, and, on a sliding scale, the Secretaries, who were last on the list, got Rs. 1,000 each.

The relations, however, between Nawab Walajah and a later Governor of Madras were not so cordial. In 1780 Haidar Ali with an immense army suddenly invaded the Carnatic, and annihilated a British force that was sent to oppose him; and Tipu, his son and successor, continued the campaign. The Company's treasury at Madras was straitened with the expenses of the war, and the Nawab, whose capital was in the hands of the enemy, was unable to contribute thereto; but when Tipu was eventually defeated, the Nawab was induced to assign the control of the revenues of the Carnatic to the Company. A few months later the Nawab felt that he had made an unwise bargain, and he declared his renunciation of the agreement; but Baron Macartney, the newly appointed Governor of Madras, kept him strictly to his word. The Nawab wrote various official letters, complaining in one that Lord Macartney had 'premeditatedly' offered him 'Insults and Indignity,' and in another that he had shown him 'every mark of Insult and Contempt.' The Directors in London, expressly declaring their desire to content the influential Nawab, decided in his favour; whereupon Lord Macartney, who in the opinion of his friends had been set at naught for the sake of the wealthy potentate, indignantly resigned the Governorship of Madras, and went home. Friendly relations between the Nawab and the Madras Government were thereupon resumed, and when Nawab Walajah died, at the age of seventy-eight, he was eulogised in an official note in the *Fort St. George Gazette.*

The career of his son and successor, Umdat-ul-Umara, was less auspicious. Although his accession was the occasion of friendly letters between himself and the Government of Madras, the Nawab's rejection of the Governor's suggestion that the financial arrangements between himself and the Company should be made more favourable to the Company irritated the Governor, and the Governor's efforts to induce the Nawab to change his mind irritated the Nawab. Meanwhile Tipu Sultan was preparing for another war with the Company, and when, after a brief campaign, Tipu was killed while fighting bravely in defence of his capital, it was declared that an examination of Tipu's correspondence showed that the Nawab of Arcot had been guilty of treasonable communications with Mysore. It was accordingly resolved that the Company should assume control of the Carnatic; but, as the Nawab was seriously ill, nothing was done until his death, when British troops were sent to occupy Chepauk Palace.

The Nawab's son refused to recognize the Company's right to control his father's dominions, whereupon the Company set him aside, and put his cousin on the throne in his stead. The Company were now the actual rulers of the Carnatic, and the future Nawabs were styled 'Titular Nawabs.' In 1855 the third of the Titular Nawabs died without any son to succeed him. Lord Dalhousie was Governor-General of India at the time, and it was Lord Dalhousie's declared policy that if the ruler of any native state died without issue, his dominions should formally lapse to the Company. On this principle the Carnatic now became a formal part of the British dominions, and the dynasty of the Nawabs came to an end; Chepauk Palace, which was the personal property of the Nawabs, was acquired by the Company's Government for a price, and was eventually turned into Government offices.

The many thousands of Mohammedans, however, who dwelt in the crowded streets and lanes of Chepauk, and who had looked upon the Nawab as their religious chief, would have been afflicted at the cessation of the Carnatic line; and after the Indian Mutiny the Government of India, respecting Mohammedan sentiment, recognized the succession of the nearest relative of the late Nawab and obtained for him from the King of England the hereditary title of Amir-i-Arcot, or 'Prince of Arcot'—an honorary title but higher than that of Nawab. A sum of Rs. 1,50,000 per annum—(not an excessive sum in relation to the revenues of the Carnatic, which are now collected by the Madras Government)—is expended annually in pensions to the Prince and to certain of his relatives; and he lives in a house called the 'Amir Mahal' (the Amir's Palace), which was given to him by the Government. The Amir Mahal stands in spacious grounds in Royapettah. At the principal entrance, the gate-house is a tall and imposing edifice in red brick. At the gateway, sentries, armed with old-fashioned rifles, stand—or sometimes sit—on guard; and the Prince's Band is often to be heard practising oriental music in the room up above.

Regarded in relation to its history, Chepauk is something more than 'one of the Government buildings on the Marina.' Let us remember that, when it was enclosed within the walls that are now no more, it was the home of Mohammedan potentates—sometimes a scene of gorgeous festivity—sometimes a scene of desperate intrigue. In imagination we may people the front garden with the gaily-uniformed Body-Guard of the Carnatic sovereign, mounted on gaily-bridled steeds; and we may see the Nawab himself coming magnificently down the front steps and climbing into the silver howdah that is strapped on the back of a kneeling elephant. A blast of oriental music, and the procession goes on its way; and we may wonder at which of the tiled windows on the upper floor the bright eyes of the Lalla Rookhs and the Nurmahals of Chepauk are slily peeping at the spectacle. The vision vanishes. The procession now is a procession of clerks to their homes when their day's work is over; and the music is a ragtime selection by the Band of the Madras Guards on the Marina, close by, with ayahs and children around. We are in the twentieth century; but for a moment we have lived in the past.

CHAPTER XI

GOVERNMENT HOUSE

In the early days of Madras all the employees of the Company, from the Governor down to the most junior apprentice, lived in common. Their bedrooms were in one and the same house, and they had their meals at one and the same table. The house stood in the middle of the Fort, and was the 'Factory'—a word which, as already explained, was used in former times to mean a mercantile office, or, as Annandale in his dictionary defines it, 'an establishment where factors in foreign countries reside to transact business for their employers;' and the Factory in Fort St. George was both an office and a home.

The community life, with the common table, was maintained for many years, but in course of time, when the number of the employees had greatly increased and some of the senior officials had wives and children, one man and another were allowed to live in separate quarters, within the precincts of the Fort; and eventually the common table, like King Arthur's, was dissolved. Even then, however, and right on until the beginning of the nineteenth century, the junior employees had a common mess, and were under something like disciplined control.

Like all the other buildings inside the Fort and within the walls of White Town, the Factory—which was sometimes spoken of as 'The Governor's House'—was without a garden; and it was only to be expected that the resident employees, most of whom were young men, should wish for a recreation ground to which they could resort in their leisure hours. Some of the wealthy private residents of White Town had shown what could be done; for they had acquired patches of land outside the walls, which they had enclosed with hedges and cultivated as gardens, with a house in the middle of each garden, in which, as either a permanent or an occasional residence, the owner and his family might hope to find relief from the stuffiness of the streets of the rapidly developing city. In the 'Records' any such villa is spoken of as a 'garden-house' and even now in Madras the term 'garden-house' is ocoasionally used in Indo-English as signifying a house that stands within its own 'compound,' as distinct from houses that open directly into the street.

The Company's agents in Madras realized the desirability of laying out a garden for the recreative benefit of the Company's employees. Outside the walls, therefore, of White Town they hedged off some eight acres of land in the locality in which the Law College now stands, and they cultivated it as a 'Company's Garden;' and within it they built a small pavilion. We may imagine that in the cool of the evening it was common for a goodly number of the Company's mercantile employees to leave their apartments in the Fort and stroll beyond the walls the short distance to the 'Garden,' which in those early days was refreshingly near the seashore. In our mind's eye we can blot the Law College out of the landscape and can see a party of youthful merchants engaged as energetically as was suitable to the heat of Madras in the then fashionable game of bowls—or, less energetically but much more excitedly, gathered in a ring round two cocks that are tearing each other to pieces—a particularly popular form of 'Sport' in old Madras; and, although the Directors in London appropriately forbade to their employees the use of cards or the dice-box, we can espy a tense-visaged quartet within the shadow of the pavilion with a 'pool' of fanams' (coins worth about 2½*d.*) on the table, or possibly, rupees ŏr pagodas, absorbed in a round of ombre or one of the other card games that were in fashion. The sun has set, and the shadows are lengthening. A bugle sounds from the Fort; and the employees stroll back to supper, which, according to an old account, invariably consisted of 'milk, salt fish, and rice,' but which will be privately supplemented afterwards with potations of arrack-punch by those who can afford nothing better and with draughts of sack or canary by those who can.

In the course of a few years the 'Company's Garden' was spoiled. Black Town had been springing up close by; and, when a wall was built round old Black Town, the Company's Garden was unpleasantly included therein, and the Garden was now in the north-west corner of the Indian city. Moreover, a part of the Garden had begun to be utilized as a European burial-ground, and huge funeral monstrosities of the bygone style had begun to dominate the enclosure.

The Company's agents in Madras felt that a new recreation-ground was a necessity; and they were agreed that there ought to be not merely a 'Company's Garden,' but a 'Company's Garden-House.' They wrote to the Directors saying that there were occasions on which the Company in Madras had to entertain 'the King (Golconda) and persons of quality,' and that they had no building that was suitable for any such ceremonial proceedings. True there was the Council Chamber in the Fort, but the Council Chamber was the place where the Company's mercantile transactions were discussed; and the Chamber, as well as all the other buildings in the Fort, was closely identified with the 'Factory;' and the Company's chief officials in Madras declared—not, we may suppose, without regard for their own convenience—that a stately 'Garden House,' unassociated with ledgers and bills of sale, ought to be built, in due accord with the stateliness of the Company itself. Their application for permission to put the work in hand was met by the Directors in London with the typically frugal reply that the work might be done but care was to be taken that the Company should be put to 'no great charge.' Possibly the representatives in Madras were able to provide additional supplies on the spot, but, however that may have been, the house was 'handsomely built,' yet 'with little expense to the Company.' The new garden seems to have comprised the area within which the Medical College and the General Hospital are now situated. The grounds, which stretched down, even as now, to the bank of the river, were well laid out, and the Company's first 'Garden House' was a fine possession.

In 1686 Master William Gyfford, Governor of Fort St. George, had a fancy for using the Garden House as a private residence for himself. It is not to be wondered at that he did so; for Master Gyfford, after twenty-seven years' residence in Madras and more than twenty-seven years in the East, was in poor health, and lately he had been taken ill with a 'a violent fitt of the Stone and Wind Collick.' The gardenless 'Factory' in the Fort was a gloomy apology for a 'Governor's House,' and the crowd of employees that were accommodated there must have been a serious infliction upon the invalid Governor; and he found the Garden House an agreeable retreat. In his new quarters he got better of his illness; and he dwelt there a considerable time, till in the following year he left Madras for England for good. The story is interesting, for it records the first occasion on which a Governor of Madras lived in a separate house outside the Fort.

On various occasions the Company's 'Garden House,' with its extensive grounds, was used for public purposes, justifying the plea for its construction. For example, when the Company received the news of the accession of King James II, the event was celebrated with brilliant proceedings at the Garden House. Similarly, at the accession of Queen Anne 'all Europeans of fashion in the City' were invited to the Garden House, where they 'drank the Queen's Health, and Prosperity to old England.' In an earlier chapter we have related how a young Nawab of Arcot who had just succeeded to his murdered father's throne was entertained at the Garden House with great doings. Governor Pitt made great developments in the Gardens, and was another Governor who liked the Garden House as a residence. An Englishman who was living in Madras in 1704, when Pitt was Governor, has left an interesting account of the Garden House as he saw it :—

> 'The Governor, during the hot Winds, retires to the Company's new Garden for refreshment, which he has made a very delightful Place of a barren one. Its costly Gates, lovely Bowling-Green, spacious Walks, Teal-pond, and Curiosities preserved in several Divisions are worthy to be Admired. Lemons and Grapes grow there, but five Shillings worth of Water and attendance will scarcely mature one of them.'

Before long it had come to be an unwritten regulation that Governors at Fort St. George might reside at their choice either in the Fort or at the Garden House. There came a time, however, when the Governor had of necessity to betake himself to the Fort; it was the time when the French were besieging Madras. During the siege the enemy used the Garden House as a vantage-ground for their big guns; and afterwards, when they had captured Fort St. George and were in occupation of the city, they pulled the Garden House down, lest the English, trying perhaps to recapture the Fort, should be able to use it as a vantage-ground in their turn.

Thus, when Madras was restored to the English, the Garden House had disappeared, and the only house for Governor Saunders was the original residence in the middle of the Fort. Governor Saunders, however, was not content with the walled-in accommodation that the

Fort provided and was unwilling to forgo the residential privileges that his predecessors had enjoyed; so a private 'garden-house' in Chepauk was rented in his behalf. It belonged to a Mrs. Madeiros, a rich Portuguese widow, whose husband, lately deceased, had been a leading merchant in White Town.

Mrs. Madeiros's house was 'Government House, Madras,' of the present day. The house, however, has been enlarged

GOVERNMENT HOUSE, MADRAS

and the grounds have been extended since Governor Saunders lived there as a tenant.

Governor Saunders liked his residence, and, before he had been there a year, the Company acquired it from the widow, who had no use for it now that her husband was dead; and the Governor was careful to leave on record the reason of the acquisition:—

> 'It having been always usual for the Company to allow the President a house in the Country to retire to, and Mrs. Medeiros being willing to dispose of her House, situated in the Road to St. Thomé, for three thousand five hundred pagodas (say Rs. 12,250). Agreed That it be purchased accordingly. The

> Company's Garden-house having been demolish'd by the French when they were in Possession of this Place, and Mrs. Medeiros's being convenient for that Purpose, and on a Survey esteem'd worth much more than the Sum 'tis offer'd at.'

The Company always enjoyed a good bargain, and Governor Saunders was justified in thinking that he had made a very good one in respect of the house; for, a few years later, the house, with certain extensions and improvements, was written down in the Company's books at a valuation of nearly four times the price that was paid for it.

We have brought our story down to the acquisition of Government House, but it remains to relate some of the historic events in which Government House has figured since it was acquired.

During the second siege of Madras by the French, under Lally, the besiegers occupied the Garden House, and during their occupation they did a great deal of wanton damage before they ceased their vain endeavours. Two years later, however, the English had the enjoyment of a delicate revenge. They captured Pondicherry and brought Lally to Madras, where they imprisoned him in the Garden House till a vessel was available to take him to England. The damage that he had done had not yet been repaired; and a contemporary Record says that 'Mr. Lally was lodged in those apartments of the Garden House which had escaped his fury at the Siege of Madras,' and that in respect of his table he was allowed to give his own orders 'without limitation of expence,' with the result that he 'seemed to have intended Revenge by Profusion.'

A few years later Tipu, Sultan of Mysore, at the head of a body of horsemen, made a sudden raid on Madras; and the troopers scampered about the well-laid-out grounds of the Garden House, looting the villages on either side. According to accounts, Governor Bourchier and his

Councillors were there when the raiders came, and they would assuredly have been caught had they not managed to make their escape in a boat that was conveniently tied up on the bank of the Cooum river.

More than one Governor of Fort St. George has died at Government House, and it was there that Governor Pigot died in extraordinary circumstances. The tale has been told in a previous chapter, that Lord Pigot was arrested by his Councillors, with whom he had quarrelled, and that he died in confinement in the Garden House.

The reader has yet to be told how the Garden House was finally transformed into the Government House that we see to-day.

In 1798 Lord Clive, son of the great Robert Clive, was sent out to India as Governor of Madras. Within the first six months of his arrival there was the excitement of a war with Mysore, in which the terrible Tipu Sultan was killed during the assault on his capital. During the tranquil remainder of his five years in India, Lord Clive turned his attention to domestic reforms, and amongst them he resolved that the Garden House should be improved. In an official minute he wrote :—

> 'The garden house, at present occupied by Myself, is so insufficient either for the private accommodation of my family and Staff, or for the convenience of the public occasions inseparable from my situation, that it is my intention to make such an addition to it as may be calculated to answer both purposes.'

Lord Clive thereupon, in 1801, developed Government House at a cost of more than Rs. 3 lakhs; and two years later he built the beautiful Banqueting Hall, at a cost of Rs. 2½ lakhs. The recent fall of Tipu's capital of Seringapatam was an event that the Banqueting Hall could appropriately commemorate; and Lord Clive, with pious respect for his dead father's memory, coupled Plassey with Seringapatam, and ordered that the fine figure-work on the façade of the hall should be a commemoration of both victories. In England the Directors of the Company complained of what they called 'such wasteful extravagance;' but the developments were a real want, and it is a matter of present-day satisfaction that the Madras Government have no need to be acquiring a site now and to be building a new Government House in these expensive days. Lord Clive was certainly no miser with the Company's money, for he built also a second Government House—a 'country residence' at Guindy. The 'country residence' was developed and improved some forty years later by Lord Elphinstone, who was Governor of Madras in the middle of last century. It is a truly beautiful house, standing in beautiful grounds; and it has lately been a proposition that the house at Guindy should be the Governor's only residence, and that Government House, Madras, should be used for Government offices.

'Government House, Madras!' To most people it is suggestive of dinner parties within and garden parties without; and the Banqueting Hall is suggestive of dances and levees and meetings for good causes. But to people who can look at Government House, Madras, with an historic glance it rouses other memories. Within its original walls more than two centuries ago a belaced Senhor kept Portuguese state. It was here that Frenchmen were encamped while their guns were fruitlessly hammering at the walls of Fort St. George. It was here that Lally lived sumptuously in prison, till he was sent to Europe—eventually to be executed in Paris for having failed to capture Madras. It was within these grounds that Tipu's horsemen were scampering about on a September morning, looking for houses where money or jewels could be commandeered. It was here that an ennobled Governor of Madras lived in gilded captivity till death set him free.

CHAPTER XII

MADRAS AND THE SEA

Madras is now a seaport of considerable repute; but it is interesting to recall the fact that less than forty years ago the city was without a harbour, and that ships which came there had to anchor out at sea. In the days of the Company, passengers and cargo had to be landed on the beach in boats; and, as the waves that chase one another to the shores of Madras are nearly always giant billows crested with foaming surf, the passage between ship and shore was not without its discomforts and also its risks.

Warren Hastings, when he was senior member of the Madras Council and was in charge of Public Works, wrote it down that he thought it 'possible to carry out a causeway or pier into the sea beyond the Surf, to which boats might come and land their goods or passengers, without being exposed to the Surf.' At various times different engineers devised plans for such a pier as Warren Hastings proposed, but nothing was actually done, and it was not until the sixties of last century that a pier was actually made. It was not a stone causeway such as Hastings seems to have had in his mind, but was a lighter and likelier structure of wood and iron; and it did excellent work, making it easy for passengers and cargo to be landed in fair weather. Madras was still, however, without a harbour; but before many years a harbour was taken in hand, and in the summer of 1881 its two arms, enclosing the small pier, were practically finished. There was much rejoicing; but the congratulations were short-lived, for on a certain night during the winter of the same year there was a cyclone off Madras, and the next morning the citizens saw that their harbour had been wrecked by the devastating waves. It was fifteen years before the harbour had been restored, upon an improved plan; and even then it was a poor apology for a haven; for when a storm was expected, ships were warned to put out to sea, as the cyclone had shown that a stormy sea was less dangerous than the storm-beaten harbour. Within recent years, however, the harbour has been so much altered and strengthened and developed that it is regarded as a splendid piece of engineering, and shipping business in Madras has benefited greatly. Large vessels can now lie up against wharves, to discharge or to load their cargo, and passengers can embark and disembark in comfort, and the increase in trade has been great. Much watchfulness, however, is still very necessary; for, on an exciting night a few years ago, part of the extended harbour-wall was washed away by a storm.

Yes, Madras is an important seaport; yet it is a fact that, except to men whose business is with the sea, Madras is much less like a seaside town than it was in its earlier years, and many of the people who live there seldom see the briny ocean—even though they may sometimes be reminded of its nearness when in the stillness of the night they hear

'The league-long breakers thundering on the shore.'

For one thing, the greater part of Madras is not so near the sea as it was in former times; for the southern wall of the harbour has acted as a breakwater, causing the sea to recede a very long way from the original shore; and houses in the thoroughfare that is still called 'Beach Road' are now a very long way from the beach, and it is only from upper stories that the sea in the distance is visible. Southward, moreover, the magnificent road that is still called the 'Marina' is fast losing its right to the name; for it is only across a broad stretch of ever-extending dry sand that the dark blue ribbon of tropical sea is beheld therefrom.

In earlier days Madras was verily a city of the sea. Both White Town and Black Town lay directly along the sea-beach, and the coming and going of the Company's ships were momentous events. Surf-boats used to land on the beach outside the 'Sea-Gate' of the wave-splashed Fort, laden with cargo from the Company's ships lying out in the roads; and the bales were carried through the

THE SEA GATE.
The sea has now receded afar.

gateway into the Company's warehouses within the Fort-walls. The Sea-Gate is still to be seen, and it still looks towards the sea; but the sea is far away, and the Sea-Gate is now one of the least used of the entrances to the Fort.

In former times the Company had a considerable fleet of first-class sailing-ships, and, owing to the frequency of wars with either the French or the Dutch, the Company obtained royal permission to equip their ships as men-of-war armed with serviceable guns, which could be turned against an enemy if occasion required. The voyage from England to India was by way of the Cape of Good Hope, and it lasted at least three or four months, and often very much more. For example, when Robert Clive came out to India for the first time, the vessel was so buffeted by contrary winds that the commander thought it best to run across the Atlantic and let her lie up so long in a South American port that Clive learned to speak Spanish with considerable fluency; and it was not till nearly a year after leaving England that the young writer arrived at Madras.

Furthermore, besides the various adventures that were natural to a sea-voyage, there was the contingency of a sea-fight, and the possibility of being taken to Pondicherry or Batavia as a prisoner of war instead of being landed at Madras as a paid employee of the 'Honourable Company.'

It was usual for several ships to sail together, for mutual protection; and passengers had reason to congratulate themselves when they were eventually landed safe and sound at Madras. It can be readily imagined that the sight of a vessel of the Company approaching in the distance caused a stir of excitement amongst the residents of Fort St. George. There were no telegraphs from other ports to give previous notice of a vessel's prospective arrival; and the fact that a ship was at hand was unknown until her flag[1] or her particular rig was discerned in the distance, or until one of her guns gave notice of her approach. The comparative regularity, however, of the winds in Eastern seas caused 'seasons' in which vessels might be expected; and

THE COMPANY'S FLAG.

[1] 'The flag displayed by the Company's ships bore seven horizontal red stripes on a white ground, with a St. George's Cross in the inner top corner.'—*Love.*

when a season arrived, the look-out who happend to be on duty on the Fort flagstaff must have been particularly alert. Ay, and there must have been much hurrying to and fro in the streets of White Town when the signal had been given and the news had spread that the sails of a Company's ship had been sighted, and while the vessel, perhaps with several consorts, came nearer and nearer, till at last the anchors were dropped and salutes were exchanged between ship and shore.

There was good cause for excitement. The ship brought letters from home—perhaps after several months of no news at all. There were the private letters that told the news about near ones and dear ones; there were the official letters that decreed appointments in the Company's service and promotions and penalties, and dealt with the Company's business; and there were the 'news-letters'—the old-fashioned predecessors of the modern newspaper, which were written by paid correspondents, whose duty it was to give their clients news of London and of England and of Europe. The news was often astounding, and was sometimes extraordinarily behind-time. For example, the Company's employees in India were still professing loyalty to the Most High and Mighty King James II nearly a twelvemonth after that monarch had fled to France and had been succeeded by William and Mary; and the employees at Madras were surprised indeed when a ship arrived one day from England with the belated news.

The salutes have been fired, and the vessel has been surrounded by a flotilla of surf-boats and catamarans. The commander and the passengers are being rowed ashore, and the Governor with his Councillors, dressed all of them in their smartest official attire, are waiting on the beach outside the Sea-Gate of the Fort to bid them a hearty welcome. Amongst the passengers there are probably some youths who have been posted to Madras either as apprenticed 'writers' or as military Cadets; and perhaps there is a senior employee who is returning to India after the rare event of a holiday in England. Possibly too there are some ladies, either wives of employees who have been willing to accompany or to follow their husbands to the mysterious East—or, as was not infrequently the case,

SURF-BOAT

young ladies who, with the consent of the Directors, have been shipped out to India by their parents or guardians or on their own account, in the hope that companionable bachelor employees, pining in their loneliness, will jump at the chance of matrimony.

The surf-boat comes nearer and nearer; and when it gets among the breakers there are feminine screams of terror. The alarm is not without cause; for at one moment the boat is being balanced on the top of a heaving wave, and the next it is almost lost to sight in a foaming hollow.

The excitement in the tossing boat is tremendous; but it is brief; for there are only three or four breakers to be negotiated, and in less than a minute a curling wave has caught the boat in its clutch and hurls it with a thud into the shallows. Naked coolies rush forward and lay hold of its sides, lest the backwash should carry it seaward again; and, with the help of the next wave, they manage to haul the boat a little further on shore, and the passengers are able to disembark—splashed, perhaps, but safe and sound.

When the greetings are over, the Governor leads the way into the Fort, where a general meal is served and the news is told and the exclamations of surprise are many. In the evening there is a banquet, and after the banquet, 'when the gentlemen have finished their wine,' and have rejoined the ladies, the stately dances of the period are 'performed;' and it is not unlikely that before the assembly breaks up, some, if not all, of the newly-arrived young ladies have received and have accepted offers of matrimony; and it is possible that two or more gallants have had a serious quarrel about this young lady or that, and even possible that, out of the Governor's sight, swords have been drawn in her regard.

On the morrow the unloading begins; and for many days a fleet of surf-boats is busily engaged in bringing ashore the broadcloths and other English wares which the Company will be able to sell at a large profit—not forgetting the barrels of canary and madeira and other luxuries that have been imported both for private consumption and also for the general table in the Fort. And when the unloading is over and the ship has been overhauled after her long voyage, the surf-boats will then be engaged in carrying to the ship the calicoes and other Indian wares that are to be exported to England for the Company's profit there.

The sea-trade of Madras is very much greater now than it was in the days of old. Not a day now passes but at least one steamship glides into the Madras Harbour, and it is always a much larger vessel than was the very largest of the sailing-ships that in those bygone times tacked laboriously to an anchorage in the Madras roads. But the excitement has disappeared. The steamers come and go with as little stir—or not so much—as when a tramcar leaves a crowded street-corner.

In Madras there are still some reminders of the times when nautical affairs were in more general evidence in Madras than they are now. For example, the 'Naval Hospital Road' is still the name of a thoroughfare which leads from the Poonamallee Road, opposite the School of Arts, to Vepery, and it is a reminder of the fact that there were once upon a time sufficient naval men in Madras to make a hospital for sick seamen a necessity. The buildings of the old Naval Hospital still exist; they are the buildings in the Poonamallee Road opposite the School of Arts. In the early part of last century the Naval Hospital itself was abolished, and the buildings were converted into a 'Gun Carriage Factory'—and this is now no more. It is a good many years indeed since the Gun Carriage Factory was closed down; and in Madras at this particular time, when there is a very pressing demand for house accommodation, many people wonder that such spacious premises in so busy a quarter of the city should have been lying idle for so long and are hoping to see them once more serving some useful purpose.

Another reminder of the nautical conditions of those days is to be found in the existence of an 'Admiralty House.' 'Admiralty House' is a fine residence in San Thomé, and is now the property of the Raja of Vizianagram. It was apparently the San Thomé residence of the Admiral of the East Indian fleet. That official had another residence within the Fort, which used also to be called 'Admiralty House'—the house which Robert Clive occupied at the time of his marriage, and which is now the Accountant-General's office.

We will glance at one more reminder of the nautical Madras of by-gone times. At Royapuram there is a large house which is now styled 'Biden House,' and is used as a harbour-masters' residence, but which until a few years ago was called 'The Biden Home' or 'The Sailors' Home.' It is not an ancient building, but it was nevertheless built in the days of the sailing-ship, and is a reminder of the times when sailing-ships used to lie out in the Madras Roads and the 'Sailors' Home' offered seamen entertainment more physically and morally wholesome than that which was provided in the low-class hotels and saloons which laid themselves out for the spoliation of Jack ashore—and of the time when the wreck of a sailing-ship on the Coromandel coast was not an uncommon occurrence and parties of distressed seamen were not infrequently to be seen in Madras, for whom a temporary 'Home' had to be provided. The 'Old Salt'—the picturesque sea-dog of sailing-ship days—has disappeared except from story-books—the old-fashioned seaman with earrings in his ears and a villainous 'quid' in his mouth, dressed in a blue jersey and the baggiest of blue trowsers, and lurching as he walked, always 'full of strange oaths', and larding his speech with nautical jargon. On shore, after a long sea-voyage, and with money in his pockets, the 'Old Salt' in an Eastern port was not always a factor for peace and progress. He was not uncommonly too frequent a visitor at what the Madras Records call the 'punch houses,' and the Records show that he often caused a disturbance. But he was a brave fellow, and at sea he did much for England's trade and for England's greatness. In an Indian seaport he was a picturesque, if troublesome, personage, and nautical Madras has changed with the Old Salt's disappearance.

CHAPTER XIII

THE STORY OF THE SCHOOLS

A tourist who goes the round of Madras must surely be impressed with the numerous signs of its educational activity. Apart from the multitude of juvenile schools in every part of the crowded city, the number of academic institutions is large, and educational buildings are amongst the most prominent of its edifices. Our tourist, putting himself in charge of a guide at the Central Station for a drive along the beautiful Marina, sees a number of academic buildings on his way. The Medical College is just outside the station yard. The classic façade of Pachaiyappa's College for Hindus peeps at him gracefully across the Esplanade. The Law College lifts its Saracenic towers above him as he passes by. Across the road he sees the collection of miniature domes and spires and towers that surmount the various buildings that make up the far-famed Christian College. Driving along the Marina he sees the Senate House of the Madras University surmounted by its four squat towers; farther on he sees the staid Engineering College, and the still staider Presidency College, and, beyond, the whitewashed buildings of Queen Mary's residential College for Women; and on his way back by the Mount Road he sees the Muhammedan College, with its little white mosque and its spacious playing-fields in the heart of the city. There are yet more colleges in Madras; and there are also numerous large schools, some of which are attended by more than a thousand pupils.

Yes, the educational activity in Madras is great; and it is interesting to reflect that it is a development from very small educational enterprises in the days when Madras was young.

The initial enterprise was small indeed. The first school in Madras was the little "public school for children, several of whom are English", which the French Capuchin priest, Father Ephraim, opened in his own house in White Town very soon after Madras came into being. His pupils were mostly Portuguese or Portuguese Eurasians, the children of Portuguese subjects who had come from Mylapore and who, for purposes of trade or commerce, had settled down within the English Company's domain. His English pupils must have been children of the very few of the Company's civil or military employees that were married, or of the still fewer English free settlers. Father Ephraim, who according to accounts was a really learned man, charged no fees, yet was deeply interested in the welfare of his scholars; and the little school must have supplied a great want in those far-off days. It is interesting indeed to think of that little 'public school;' for the room in the priest's house was the scene of the very first beginning of what are now the mighty educational activities of Madras—an earnest, moreover, of the great things that the Roman Catholic Church was going to do in the way of education, both for boys and for girls, in South India.

Father Ephraim's school continued to prosper under his successors, and in the seventeenth century it was transferred, as a poor-school, to a building in the grounds of what is now the Roman Catholic Cathedral in Armenian Street; and in 1875 it was put under the control of the brothers of St. Patrick, an Irish order of educational monks, and it became St. Patrick's orphanage. Later the brothers transferred themselves and their orphanage to the spacious park—Elphinstone Park—on the southern bank of the Adyar River, the premises which they occupy still.

For some thirty years the Company took no part in

educational work, and the children of Madras were left entirely to Father Ephraim's care. Then for two years a certain Master Patrick Warner was the Company's temporary chaplain of Madras—a conscientious and uncompromising Protestant minister who wrote some long letters to the Directors in England denouncing the laxity of the conduct of the Company's employees and deploring the influence that Roman Catholic priests had been allowed to obtain in Fort St. George. Finally, he went back to England, with the threat that he was going to interview the Directors on various matters pertaining to Madras; and that he succeeded in making himself heard is to be seen in the fact that in the following year the Directors sent a Protestant schoolmaster out to Madras. The letter in which they notified the appointment to the Governor in Council at Fort St. George was assuredly inspired by Master Patrick Warner's undoubtedly high-minded representations. They wrote that, as there were now in Fort St. George 'so many married families,' they were sending out 'one Mr. Ralph Orde to be schoolmaster at the Fort '. . . who is to teach all the Children to read English and to 'write and Cypher gratis, and if any of the other Natives, 'as Portuguez, Gentues (Telugus),[1] or others will send their 'Children to School, we require they be also taught gratis '. . . and he is likewise to instruct them in the Principles of 'the Protestant religion.' Mr. Ralph Orde arrived by the same ship which brought the letter, and his arrival (1677) is another notable event in the history of education in Madras. It was the first beginning of Government education—the laying of the first stone in what is now such a vast edifice.

In appointing a schoolmaster, the Directors meant to do their best for education in their rising city; for they had

[1] In modern Madras the great majority of the Hindu residents are Tamils; but in the beginning there were very few Tamil immigrants, and the Hindu residents were nearly all of them Telugus (Gentoos).

engaged no mean dominie on a menial's pay. In choosing Mr. Ralph Orde they chose a good man, and they paid him accordingly. He was to dine at the General Table, and his salary was to be £50 a year, which in those days was no small sum—more than the salary of some of the Members of Council. Perhaps, indeed, they got too good a man for the post; for after five years of educational work in Madras, Mr. Orde complained that his schoolmastering had been 'much prejudicial to my health,' and he asked to be relieved of his duties and to be appointed to a post in the Company's civil service instead. His request was granted. A new schoolmaster was appointed; and as a 'Civilian' Mr. Orde worked with such success that in two or three years he was sent to Sumatra to be the Chief of a factory that he was to found on the west coast of the island. The ex-schoolmaster would, perhaps, have risen to be Governor of Madras, but it would seem that life in the East had really been 'much prejudicial to his health,' for he died in Sumatra ten years after his first arrival in Madras.

In 1688, by virtue of the Company's Royal Charter, a Corporation of the City of Madras came into being, and it was among their delegated duties that they should build a school in Black Town for the purpose of teaching 'Native children to speak, read, and write the English Tongue, and to understand Arithmetic and Merchants' Accompts.' Three years later, however, Elihu Yale, Governor of Madras, complained to the Corporation that, although they had been empowered to levy taxes on the citizens, they had not so much as thought about building a school, and had neglected various other civic responsibilities. The Company—rightly or wrongly—sought to justify their inaction with the excuse which the Corporation of Madras has—rightly or wrongly—made for civic inaction so many times since, namely that 'no funds' had been assigned to them by Government for the works that they were called upon to undertake. As for taxation, they remarked that the people in Black Town had not been schooled to civic taxation; and it is true that any ruthless collection of taxes might have meant wholesale departures from the city, or at any rate a serious check to further immigration. So the municipal school for Native children never came into being.

Meanwhile the Company's free school in White Town, started by Mr. Orde, continued its work under Mr. Orde's successors; and elementary instruction was imparted therein to a heterogeneous crowd of children—English, Eurasians, and Indians—Christians and Hindus. Eventually the school was put in charge of the chaplain of St. Mary's Church in the Fort, and the chaplain and his churchwardens agreed in thinking that such education was not of the kind that a Church should control, and that it was rather their duty to institute in Madras a residential free-school for poor Protestant children of British descent, which should be conducted on the lines of the many 'charity schools' in England; and in 1715, with the approval of the Directors, 'St. Mary's Church Charity School' was founded. The event is of particular interest; for St. Mary's Church Charity School developed later into the 'Male Asylum'—the institution which has done so much for boys and girls for so many years, and which, after changing its habitation on various occasions, is now comfortably housed in spacious premises in the Poonamallee road.

The year 1715 is noteworthy on another account. St. Mary's School having been founded solely for the benefit of children of European descent, the native children who had attended the Company's day-school were deprived of education. The Society for the Promotion of Christian Knowledge undertook to supply the want, by establishing schools in Madras for the special benefit of Indian children; and the year 1715, therefore, is the date which marks the first beginning of the educational work that English Protestant missionary societies have done in India. The Society found themselves unable to take up the work immediately themselves; so they applied to the vigorous Danish Lutheran Mission at Tranquebar, which was then a Danish settlement; and a Danish minister was sent to Madras to set things going.

In the course of time Madras had become a much more habitable city than it had been in its first beginnings, and a much more possible place of residence for European women. The Company's employees, therefore, were more and more disposed to matrimony; and, as already related, the Directors, believing that married men made steadier employees, had from early times encouraged the nuptial humour by sending out from England periodical batches of well-connected young women as prospective brides for employees who lacked either the means or the inclination to take a trip home to choose partners for themselves. The number of European fathers and mothers, therefore, in Madras was continually increasing; and for the education of their children, as also for that of children of well-to-do Eurasians, there was need of a different kind of education than the various free-schools supplied. Home education, with or without paid tutors and governesses, probably served its turn with some, but it was certain that sooner or later the private school would come into being.

We are unable to say when the first private school in Madras was started; but an advertisement in one of the issues of the *Madras Courier*, in 1790, shows that a private school for boys was started in that year; and it was probably the first. The enterprising educationist was Mr. John Holmes, M.A., who opened the 'Madras Academy' in Black Town for the instruction of boys in 'Reading, Writing, Arithmetic, History, the use of the Globes, French, Greek, and Latin.' Other towns in the Madras Presidency had their English residents, so Mr. Holmes offered to accommodate 'a few Boarders;' and the offer was found so convenient that certain parents wanted accommodation for their girls as well as for their boys. Mr. Holmes was willing to receive all the pupils that he could get; for in an advertisement two months later he announced that he was going to move to a larger house in which 'apartments will be allotted for the Young Ladies entirely removed and separate from the Young Gentlemen.'

The Madras Academy was eminently successful; but the mixed boarding school was not its most commendable side; and in the following year an enterprising lady-educationist announced that she was opening in Black Town a 'Female Boarding School,' in which her young ladies would be 'genteelly boarded, tenderly treated, carefully Educated, and the most strict attention paid to their Morals,' and the school was to be conducted as far as possible 'in the manner most approv'd of in England.' The enterprising lady-educationist was a Mrs. Murray, who had been a mistress in the Female Asylum. Her syllabus of education was of a more feminine sort than that which was followed at the Madras Academy; for, as announced in the prospectus, it included 'Reading and Writing, the English language and Arithmetic; Music, French, Drawing and Dancing; with Lace, Tambour, and Embroidery, all sorts of Plain and Flowered needle-work.' The two syllabuses are interesting reminders as to what were the usual subjects of education for European boys and girls a century and a half ago.

Schools, therefore, were available for children of every class—European and Indian, rich and poor; but the schools for Indians, conducted either by missionaries or by indigenous teachers, were of an elementary kind; and, apart from Oriental studies in indigenous institutions, there was little or nothing in the way of higher education for

Indians either in Madras or anywhere else in India. This condition was altered, however, during the governorship of Lord William Bentinck, the magnanimous if not brilliant governor-general whose term of office lasted for seven years, from 1828 to 1835.

During this period everything favoured educational progress in India. There was peace in England and there was peace in India. It was a time of great educational developments in England, as is manifested by the fact that within this period the London University and Durham University were opened, and the great British Association for the Advancement of Science was established. Such conditions in England had their influence in India, and the more so because Lord William Bentinck was ardent for progress. The opening of the Madras Medical College in 1835 was one of the signs of the times. During Lord William Bentinck's term of office education in India was reformed. Macaulay, afterwards Lord Macaulay, was an Indian official at the time, and he penned a notable report on education in India, in which he belittled vernacular learning and asserted that the Government of India would do well to discountenance it altogether, and to introduce western learning and the study of English literature into all schools under Government control, and to make it a rule that the English language was to be the only medium of instruction. Whether or not Macaulay's views were correct, they were adopted by the Government of India, and Lord William Bentinck issued in 1835 a resolution in accordance therewith, in which he sought to secure the people's acceptance of English education for their children by notifying that a knowledge of English would in future be necessary for admission into Government service. Government service is particularly coveted in India, and the resolution encouraged the foundation of schools of a good class in which special attention would be given to the study of the English language; and within a few years a number of important educational institutions had been founded in different parts of India.

In South India the Madras Christian College, called originally 'The General Assembly's Institution,' was first in the field. It was founded in 1837, by the Rev. John Anderson, the first missionary that the Church of Scotland sent out to Madras. The name of the founder is preserved in the 'Anderson Hall' in one of the college buildings; but the remarkable progress of the institution has been very specially due to the untiring energy of the Rev. Dr. Miller, whose statue stands on the opposite side of the public road. Dr. Miller was Principal for a number of years, and now (1921) at a great age the venerable educationist is living in retirement in Scotland.

In 1839, two years after the foundation of the Christian College, the Roman Catholic Bishop in Madras, Dr. Carew, founded St. Mary's Seminary, which after forty-five years became St. Mary's College, and which is now represented by St. Mary's High School for Europeans and St. Gabriel's High School for Indians.

Two years later, in 1841, the Presidency College had its beginning, in a rented room in Egmore. At its foundation it was not a Government institution, but was a public school under the control of governors, who were chosen from among the leading Europeans and Indians in Madras, with the Advocate-General as their first president. It was styled 'The High School of the Madras University,' and it was the founders' intention that when a college department had been added, the institution should be called the 'Madras University,' and should apply for a charter. In the sixties, however, the Madras Government was considering a scheme of its own for a University of Madras, whereupon the governors of the 'University High School' transferred their school to the Government, who called it the 'Presidency College.' The Presidency College continued to work in the rented building until 1870, when the building that it now occupies was publicly opened by the Duke of Edinburgh.

Pachaiyappa's College, a well-known Hindu institution, had its first beginning in 1842. Like the other colleges in Madras, it began as a school; the school was called

UNIVERSITY SENATE HOUSE

'Pachaiyappa's Central Institution,' and was located in Black Town. The present buildings were opened in 1850 by Sir Henry Pottinger, an ex-governor of Madras, amid a large gathering of leading European and Indian residents; and for a number of years the annual 'Day' at Pachaiyappa's College was an important social event. Pachaiyappa was a rich and religious Hindu, who made his money as a broker in the Company's service, and who died more than a hundred years ago leaving a lakh of pagodas—some $3\frac{1}{2}$ lakhs of rupees—for temple purposes. The trustees neglected the provisinns of the will, whereupon the High Court assumed control of the funds, which under the Court's control rose to the value of nearly Rs. 7½ lakhs. The original amount was set apart for the fulfilment of the terms of the

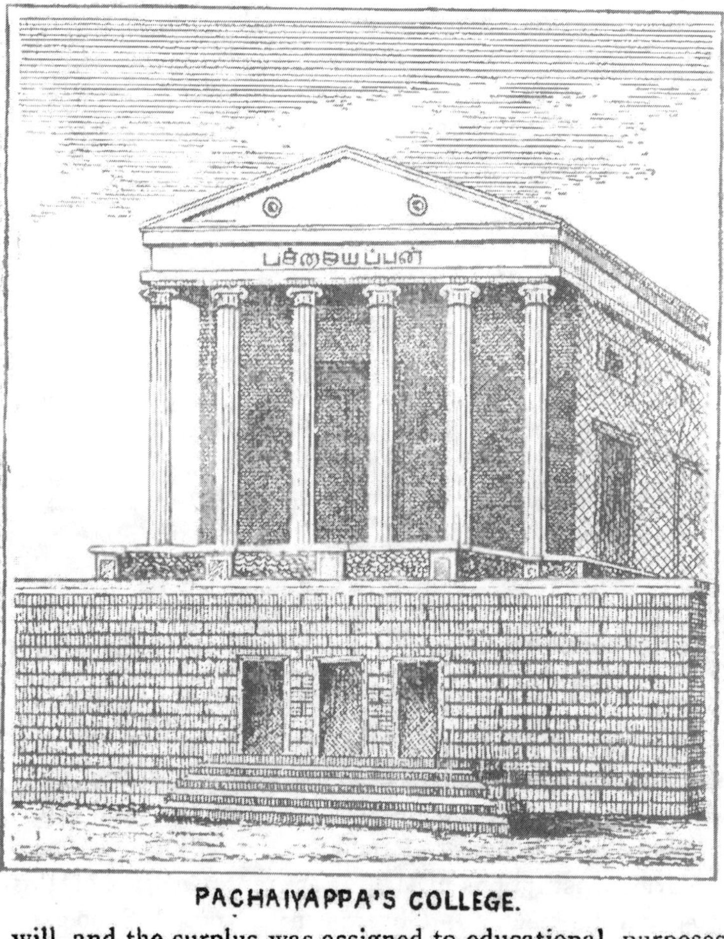

PACHAIYAPPA'S COLLEGE.

will, and the surplus was assigned to educational purposes in Pachaiyappa's name.

The education of girls shared in the development; for in 1842 the first party of Nuns of the Presentation Order was brought out from Ireland, and a convent, with a boarding school and an orphanage,—the 'Georgetown Convent'

7

of to-day—was established in Black Town. The 'Vepery Convent School' and some of the other successful convent schools in Madras are controlled by nuns of the same Order.

Education in India was given further impetus in the time of Lord Dalhousie. During his term of office (1848-1856) the present system of education, under a Director of Public Instruction, was introduced, and Government was

DOVETON PROTESTANT COLLEGE

empowered to make liberal educational grants, and to establish universities. The despatch in which the educational developments were announced has been called 'the intellectual charter of India.'

Various institutions in Madras are representative of this later development. A Government 'Normal School'—which has grown into the 'Teachers' College of to-day—was established in 1856, to increase the number and the efficiency of indigenous teachers; and the Madras University was incorporated in 1857, for the control and the development of higher education. Of large high schools still existing, the Harris High School in Royapettah was founded by the Church Missionary Society in 1856, for the education of Mohammedan boys, and was named after Lord Harris, who was Governor of Madras at the time; and the Hindu High School, in Triplicane, was founded in 1857. Doveton College, Vepery, for Anglo-Indian boys was opened in 1855. It owes its existence to a wealthy Eurasian, Captain John Doveton, who obtained his Captaincy in the service of the Nizam of Hyderabad, and who left a large sum of money to an earlier institution, the Parental Academy, which was afterwards called Doveton College in the deceased officer's honour. Within later years philanthropic and enterprising Indians have done much for education, and numerous schools both for boys and for girls have been established by their efforts.

An educational building of curious interest is the office of the Director of Public Instruction, in Nungumbaukam. It is commonly known as the 'Old College'. In the masonry of a large arch at the entrance, as well as on another arch within, quaint designs have been introduced—mysterious faces, and flags, and strange geometrical figures. The house was the property of a wealthy Armenian merchant named Moorat, who died more than a hundred years ago; and it may be supposed that the quaint designs were after the nature of family memorials. In the early part of last century the Armenian merchant's son sold the building to Government, who used it as a 'College for Junior Civilians.' Hence the designation 'Old College'; but the name does not mean that it was a building in which young civilians were trained, but means that it was a building in which there were 'colleagues' in residence, or, in other words, that, the 'General Table' having been dissolved, the 'College' was a mess-house for junior civilians. Later, its large hall was for many years a recognized assembly-room for amateur concerts, amateur dramatic entertainments, and other occasions of social reunion. The quaint devices on the gates are still preserved, and the name of the old 'College' still survives; but the associations have gone. Not even as a ghost does the long-robed Armenian merchant tread the floors; the junior civilians, with their ancient pranks and their antiquated jests, have departed; in the great hall the lilt of the song and the frenzy of the fiddles for the dance and the amateur mouthings of the drama are heard no more. A multitude of turbanned clerks are pouring forth the blue-black ink from their pens; schoolmasters haunt the portals to press their claims for educational grants for their own particular schools; and the click of a chorus of typewriters is the only music that is borne upon the breeze.

I have told the story of the schools. It is creditable to Madras; for great things have been done since that first little 'public school' was opened in the Fort.

CHAPTER XIV

HERE AND THERE

Before closing the story of Madras, it will be well to speak, at least very briefly, of some of the prominent landmarks of the city that we have not yet described.

Of churches, we should mention St. George's Cathedral. It was opened in 1816, not as a cathedral but as an ordinary church; for Madras then was not a diocese by itself, but was a part of the immense diocese of Calcutta. The new church was regarded as a necessity; for a great many 'garden houses' had sprung up in and about the Mount Road, in the area that was called the 'Choultry Plain,' and the Directors of the Company agreed with representations from Madras that it was undesirable that English residents within the bounds should be able to stay away from the Church-services on Sunday with the reasonable excuse that the nearest Anglican church—St. Mary's in the Fort—was too far away from their houses for them to be expected to attend. So the new church was built; and some twenty years later, when Dr. Corrie, Archdeacon of Calcutta, was consecrated first Bishop of Madras, the church became 'the Cathedral Church of St. George.' St. George's Cathedral is a stately building, with a spire 139 feet high, and it stands in spacious grounds. The total cost was more than two lakhs of rupees; but nobody had to be asked to subscribe, for the money was available from a peculiar source. It was an age in which State lotteries were in vogue; Madras had followed the fashion with a series of official lotteries, and a 'Lottery Fund' had been created from the profits, so that there was always a good supply of cash available for extraordinary expenses, such as mending the roads or entertaining distinguished visitors. It was from the Lottery Fund that the cost of building St. George's was met.

St. Andrew's Church—most commonly known as 'The Kirk'—was planned while St. George's was being built; and it is remarkable that it was not projected

ST GEORGE'S CATHEDRAL.

sooner than it was. Scotchmen in Madras, as in other parts of India, apart from Scottish soldiers, have been many; and the names of a number of Madras roads and houses—such as Anderson Road, Graeme's Road, Davidson Street, Brodie Castle, Leith Castle, Mackay's Gardens—are reminders of the fact that not a few of the Scots of Madras have been influential; and at the time when a second Anglican church was being built in the city it was suggested to the Directors of the Company in

England that the numerous residents who were members of the Church of Scotland ought to have a church too. The Directors, who realized no doubt the desirability of being agreeable to the many Scots in Madras, one of whom at the time was the Governor himself, Mr. Hugh Elliot, consented to the suggestion, and in 1815 they sent out a notification that a Presbyterian church was to be built not only

ST. ANDREW'S (THE "KIRK").

at Madras but also in each of the other Presidency cities at the Company's expense, and that the Company would maintain a Presbyterian chaplain at each. The Directors laid down no instructions as to what was to be the maximum cost of each kirk, but it was unpretentious buildings that they had in mind. At Bombay a large kirk was built for less than half a lakh of rupees, but for the kirk at Madras the Madras Government submitted a bill for nearly Rs. 2¼ lakhs—some Rs. 10,000 more than the total cost of St. George's Cathedral, and the Directors were indignant. The Kirk, however, had been built; and it is one of the handsome churches of Madras.[1] It is a domed building, with a tall steeple over the Grecian façade; and some of its critics have said that the combination of dome and steeple gives the edifice a strangely camel-backed appearance; but, however that may be, the dome adds beauty to the interior. When the Church was opened, it was found that the dome evoked disturbing echoes, and a large additional expense had to be incurred to exorcise the wandering voices. The steeple reaches a height of 166½ feet, which is 27½ feet higher than that of St. George's.

The Roman Catholic Cathedral at Mylapore has been described on page 61. A sketch of the handsome building is given on the next page.

The High Court, a red Saracenic structure that spreads itself out over a large area between Georgetown and the Fort, is a modern building. It was opened within the memory of elderly lawyers of Madras, some of whom used themselves to practise in the big building which is now the Collector's Office, opposite the gate of the Port Trust premises, and which was for many years the habitation of the Supreme Court at Madras. The present High Court is a mighty monument to the development of 'The Law' in Madras. In the early days of Fort St. George the Company administered its own justice to its own people, and the court was held in a building in the Fort. Punishments in those far-off times, judicial or otherwise, were

[1] Major de Haviland, of the Madras Engineers, built St. George's on a plan designed by Major Caldwell, his senior in the service. Major de Haviland both designed the Kirk and built it, and he devoted himself to his work and was very proud of his creation, which was nevertheless much criticized by unfriendly critics.

usually severe; and the Records show that even a civil servant of junior rank who gave trouble was liable to be awarded some such penalty as to sit for an hour or more on a sharp-backed 'wooden horse,' with or without weights attached to the delinquent's feet. In the town that grew up outside the Fort, justice as between natives of the soil was administered by an Indian *adikhari*, who

ST. THOMÉ CATHEDRAL.

represented the lord of the soil. As the Company's influence and authority increased, various courts of law were created—and the Records show that there were certainly crimes enough to justify their creation. A large number of the criminal trials in the earlier years of Madras were in respect of thefts of children, to sell them as slaves, especially to Dutch merchants along the coast, where the victims were not likely to be traced. Slavery was a recognized condition of life in old Madras, as indeed it was in the whole of Europe; and in the Council-book of Fort St. George there is still to be seen an Order, dated

September 29, 1687, "that Mr. Fraser do buy fforty young Sound Slaves for the Rt. Hon'ble Company," who were to be made to work as boatmen in the Company's fleet of surf-boats. It was in reference to a slave that the first case of trial by jury was held in Madras, in 1665, and it was a *cause célèbre*. The prisoner was a Mrs. Dawes, who was accused of having murdered a slave girl in her service. The Governor himself, who, like a doge of Venice, was both ruler and judge, was on the bench, and the twelve jurymen gave a unanimous verdict that Mrs. Dawes was 'guilty of the murther, but not in mannere and forme,' by which they seem to have meant that the circumstances of the case exonerated her from the capital charge. Being pressed to give a verdict 'without exception or limitation,' they brought in a unanimous verdict of 'not guilty,' whereupon the Governor felt that, although the woman had been guilty of a crime, he had no help for it but to set her free. He thereupon wrote to the Directors in England, expressing his disapproval of 'such an unexpected verdict,' and notifying that in his ignorance of the law and its formalities he was by no means confident that he had done the right thing; and the end of it was that the Governor, presumably with the Directors' approval, created two justices, on whom was thereafter to fall the responsibility of hearing all such serious cases. Change upon change! and to-day the Madras High Court, with the various other courts in different parts of the city, is a very visible symbol of the serious reality of the administration of justice.

The story of the origin of the principal literary and scientific institutions in Madras is interesting. In the olden times, when there were no literary or scientific magazines by which an 'exile in the East' could keep himself in touch with the developments of genius throughout the world, people in India with literary or scientific tastes had to be content to gratify their tastes with local researches, and to depend upon one another for any interchange of ideas. This meant that old-time literary and scientific societies in India were naturally more enthusiastic than most such societies in India are now. Madras indeed has been particularly fortunate in her time in having had residents who were earnest in cultured pursuits, and whose work survives, directly or indirectly, at the present day.

For example, it was an old-time Madras Civilian, with a hobby for astronomy and with a private observatory of his own, that created a local interest in the science and is thereby to be regarded as the originator of the Madras Observatory—the first British Observatory in the East, a famous institution in olden days, which secured for Madras the honour—which is still hers—of setting the standard of time throughout the whole of India. The Madras Civilian was Mr. William Petrie, an extraordinarily versatile genius, who entered the service as a young man and rose to be a member of the Government, yet managed to find time for very serious astronomical pursuits in his house at Nungambaukam. Going home to England on long furlough, Mr. Petrie allowed the Madras Government to acquire his instruments; and in 1791, when he came back to Madras, the Madras Observatory was built, with Mr. Petrie as adviser.

Another enthusiastic scientist in Madras in the same period was Dr. James Anderson, who, after many years of work in the Company's medical service, settled down at Madras as 'Physician-General,' on a salary of £2,500 a year, and devoted himself and a large part of his handsome salary to botanical pursuits. He acquired in Nungambaukam more than a hundred acres of land, which included what are now the grounds of the houses that go by the names of Pycroft's Gardens and Tulloch's Gardens; and for nearly a quarter of a century, until his death, Dr. Anderson utilized his leisure in the creation and development of a useful and ornamental botanical garden. He was most enthusiastic over his hobby, and he was continually carrying out botanical and agricultural experiments, of medical or commercial or industrial value. His grounds were open to the public, and 'Dr. Anderson's Botanical Gardens' became famous, and were a place of popular resort. Dr. Anderson died at the age of seventy-two; and in St. George's Cathedral his memory is graced with a fine statue that was carved by the most eminent sculptor, Sir Francis Chantrey, and for which his medical brethren in the Madras Service subscribed. How many years after his death his gardens continued to exist it might be difficult to say, but they must have suffered badly from the want of the ardent botanist's enthusiastic care. But the botanic spirit that Dr. Anderson had started remained alive in Madras; for in 1835, when, to the regret of many, his gardens had been split up into building-sites for two private residences, there was still a sufficient number of botanically inclined people in the city to found the Agri-Horticultural Society of Madras, a still-energetic body whose beautiful gardens at Teynampet deserve to be more generally appreciated by the public than they are.

The Madras Literary Society was founded a good many years ago. Its work now is that of a circulating library; but in earlier times it was especially a 'literary society,' and its meetings, at which lectures were delivered or papers were read and discussed, were crowded gatherings of the leading Europeans in the city. The original Literary Society included scientific researches within its scope, and scientific members used to discourse learnedly on scientific subjects of topical interest, such as 'The Land-Crabs of Madras,' or 'Prehistoric Tombs in the Salem District,' or 'Gold in the Wynaad of Malabar.' The name of the Society remains, but the literary and scientific meetings are no more. The last lecture, if memory fails not, was delivered in the nineties, and the audience was not large enough or enthusiastic enough to denote that lectures were any longer in demand. As a 'Literary Society and Auxiliary of the Royal Asiatic Society,' the institution has outlived its requirement; but it has a valuable store of more than 50,000 books, new and old, on all subjects, and it is continually adding to the number; and, as a circulating library of a high standard, it fulfils an excellent literary purpose.

The Madras Museum is a magnificent institution. It is to the Madras Literary Society that it owes its being; and the Literary Society did Madras splendid service in the initiation thereof. This was in 1851, when the Literary Society presented its fine collection of geological specimens to the Madras Government as the nucleus of the rich and varied store of treasures that the Madras Museum now displays. The Government lodged the geological specimens in the 'Collector's Cutcherry'—a house which forms a part—the oldest part—of the Museum buildings of to-day. Before the Government acquired the house in 1830 for a Cutcherry, the house had been private property, and, under the name of the 'Pantheon,' it had been for many years the predecessor of the Old College as the 'Assembly Rooms', wherein Madras Society had its balls, its plays, and its big dinners. The name of the old building still survives in the Pantheon Road, in which the Museum is situated.

A high circular building on the Marina always attracts a stranger's attention. It has a curious and interesting history. It is commonly called 'The Ice-House,' and the name suggests its original purpose. A number of years ago, when ice-factories had not been started and when in Madras the luxury of the 'cool drink' was unknown, somebody conceived the idea of importing ship-loads of blocks of ice from America. The idea was developed, and about the year 1840 a commercial scheme took shape. A large circular building was erected close to the sea-beach as a reservoir for the imported ice, which sailing-ships brought in huge blocks from the western world; and for a number of years the scheme was a commercial success. The ice was sold at four annas a pound, and many people in Madras remember the time when it was the only ice that was to be had, and large quantities of it were sold. With the eventual institution of ice-factories, which could supply ice at a much cheaper rate, the enterprise came to an end, and for a considerable time the ice-reservoir was out of use. Then somebody bought it, and put windows into the walls, and turned it into a residence; and meanwhile, as a result of the construction of the harbour, the sea receded a long way down the Ice-house shore. As a residence, however, a house of so strange a shape was not in request; and eventually some benevolent Hindus turned it into a free hostel for any preacher or religious teacher of repute, whatever his creed, who might be temporarily staying in Madras, especially if he felt that he had a message to deliver to the city. But the reputable prophets who availed themselves of the proffered hospitality were few; and the 'Ice-house' had a deserted look. A few years ago the Madras Government acquired it for the excellent purpose of a 'Brahman Widows' Home' for Brahman girl-widows at school. This is the purpose that it now fulfils. From Ice-house to child-widows' home! It is a great transformation—from a house whose chambers were stored with hard blocks of cold ice to a house whose chambers are aglow with the warmth of young life! There is room to hope that in course of time the Child-widows' Home will have outlived its purpose—in the time when gentler ideals will prevail, and the sorrows of child-widows will have ceased, and the institution will no longer be a need.

CHAPTER XV

'NO MEAN CITY'

It is less than three hundred years since Mr. Francis Day, seeking a likely spot for a trading settlement, surveyed the desolate sea-beach near the mouth of the Cooum, and decided that the settlement should be there. A few scattered huts on the shore and a few catamarans out at sea were the only signs of human life, and the breakers that sported on the beach were the only manifestations of activity. But the years have gone by—wild times and quiet times, years of war and years of peaceful progress—and the scene has changed, and great is the transformation. In place of the scattered huts there are huge buildings on the beach, and behind them is a great and ever greater city. The catamarans have not disappeared, but great ships pass to and fro in the offing or lie within the shelter of the harbour walls. The little 'Factory' in the Fort, within which the Company transacted its mercantile business, has gone; but elsewhere in its stead there are big offices of numerous commercial firms; and, moreover, there are large 'factories' of the modern kind, such as are denoted by tall chimneys and the perpetual roar of whirring wheels.

The growth of Madras is a remarkable testimony to British enterprise, energy, and perseverance, and also to Indian appreciation of the new-comers and of their methods; and it is a matter of satisfaction that many illustrious Indians have played an energetic and conspicuous part in the development of the city and the promotion of its welfare. In many respects the conditions were altogether unfavourable for the foundation of a maritime city. There was no natural harbour, and the breakers beat continually on the shore; and the so-called river was of little practical use. The nearest Indian towns were a good many miles away, and the Portuguese merchants in the neighbouring settlement of Mylapore were commercial rivals, who might have been supposed to have absorbed all the trade that was to be had. Yet Madras is now a large city, with more than half a million inhabitants; and its commerce and its industries have been so successful that its population is still increasing rapidly. Houses are being built everywhere, yet the demand increases. Not only are the suburbs being extended, but moreover the gardens of existing houses are being everywhere divided, so as to provide further building-sites; and two houses or more now stand within grounds that were formerly occupied by only one.

But it is well for Madras that, except in respect of some of its streets and particular localities, it is not a crowded city, and that there is therefore room for such additions. Madras has been called the 'City of Distances,' and it still deserves the name; for within its limits there are some magnificent spaces, and in the garden of many a private house the resident can sit of an evening and imagine himself in a rural retreat, far from the madding crowd.

Like all cities, Madras has its drab—very drab!—quarters and its mean—very mean!—and straggling streets. Madras was not laid out on any definite plan. Like ancient Rome, it had in the beginning to attract outsiders to come and live there, and outsiders had to be given much license to do things their own way, and the city was allowed to grow just as it would; and in respect of many of its parts there is much room for criticism. But Madras is a fine city nevertheless, with a number of stately buildings, both public and private, and with great possibilities; and its 'Marina' can truly be called magnificent.

But the greatest charm of Madras lies in its history. It was here that the foundations of the Indian Empire may be said to have been laid. The history of Madras is not a story of aggressive warfare. The settlers were gentle merchants, whose weapon was not the sword but the pen, and whose only desire it was to be left alone to carry on their business in peace. But the rising city was a continual mark for the hostility of commercial and political rivals, both European and Indian. It was a storm-centre, and the storms were often fierce; and the merchants were often compelled to meet force with force. Moreover, the merchants were men, and their doings therefore were by no means always without reproach; but, with due allowance for human weakness, the history of Madras is a history of which Madras may be proud. The city has grown from strength to strength, and in its story there is much inspiration. This little book has merely told the story in part; but it will have served its purpose if it has in any way helped the reader to realize that the story of Madras is the story of no mean city.

INDEX

The figures refer to the pages